Richard Flanagan's novels *Death of a River Guide*, *The Sound of One Hand Clapping*, *Gould's Book of Fish*, *The Unknown Terrorist* and *Wanting* are published in twenty-six countries. He directed the feature film version of *The Sound of One Hand Clapping*. A rapid on the Franklin River, Flanagan's Surprise, is named after him.

ALSO BY RICHARD FLANAGAN

Death of a River Guide
The Sound of One Hand Clapping
Gould's Book of Fish
The Unknown Terrorist
Wanting

And what do you do, Mr Gable?

Short pieces by Richard Flanagan

VINTAGE BOOKS

Australia

A Vintage book
Published by Random House Australia Pty Ltd
Level 3, 100 Pacific Highway, North Sydney NSW 2060
www.randomhouse.com.au

First published by Vintage in 2011

Addresses for companies within the Random House Group can
be found at www.randomhouse.com.au/offices

National Library of Australia
Cataloguing-in-Publication Entry

Flanagan, Richard, 1961–
And what do you do, Mr Gable?/Richard Flanagan.

ISBN 978 1 74275 272 3 (pbk.)

A823.3

Cover design by Design by Committee
Internal design by Midland Typesetters
Typeset in 11/14.5 Plantin by Midland Typesetters, Australia
Printed and bound by Griffin Press, an acredited ISO AS/NZS
14001:2004 Environmental Management System printer

10 9 8 7 6 5 4 3 2 1

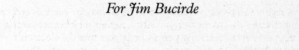

For Jim Bucirde

Remember, too, that in literature you always lose, but the difference, the enormous difference, lies in losing while standing tall, with eyes open, not kneeling in a corner praying to Jude the Apostle with chattering teeth.

Roberto Bolaño

I like books that smell of sweat.

Gustave Flaubert

Contents

Out of a Wild Sea

I DON'T DRINK of a morning. Not normally. Truth be known, I don't feel the need to drink, not like I once knew the need. And I hadn't meant to be getting drunk that morning. But outside it was a dismal winter's day, and inside the kitchen table miraculously filled with old friends and then food and then bottles, and it steamed with warmth and it smelt of yeast, and none of us had seen each other for such a long time that the only thing flowing more freely than the drink were the stories. Jamma McLeod told a tale about a young man who was discovered in the hugeness of D'Entrecasteaux Channel, heading for the open sea. The young man was in a dinghy with only a bread knife and a loaf of bread, dressed as Desdemona, intending to row the forlorn four hundred miles of ocean that lies between Hobart and Australia, because he thought Tasmania was crappy.

I knew a bloke once who tried to do it without a bread knife, said Pig Cranwell.

Everyone laughed. Even me. Even though I was the bloke without the bread knife.

I don't really know why Jim and I wanted to kayak Bass Strait. Sam Jooste was getting married in Sydney and he was our mate, with all that such things meant, and we couldn't afford an aeroplane ticket. We thought we would just kayak the Strait, then hitch from Victoria up to Sydney. At the very least it was a good joke, and consistent with our behaviour to that point, which had established us as people who would kayak any rapid on any river, no matter how big and threatening. A local newspaper ran a photo of us shooting Cataract Gorge in flood with the caption, The Suicide Twins. That was also a good joke. Some said we had a death wish, but I don't think it was the case.

We had one book with us on the trip, Saul Bellow's *Henderson the Rain King*. It begins like this: 'What made me take this trip to Africa? There is no quick explanation. Things got worse and worse and worse and pretty soon they were too complicated.' Henderson has a disturbance in his heart, a voice that constantly says 'I want, I want, I want', but what it wants it knows not. Maybe it was like that. On the other hand, maybe if we had a different book, maybe we would have thought about the whole thing differently. I don't know.

Maybe if the weather had been different we would have made it. No one had predicted anything like the force-nine gale that turned a calm ocean into a liquid earthquake. The sea grew huge, the waves breaking at the top of their great peaks, crashing into nothingness, to once more rear up as vast molten mountains.

After a time, our initial grim determination gave way to a terrified despair. At some stage we must have realised we might not make it. We activated our emergency radio distress beacon. We may have set off our flares. I can't remember. Nothing happened. No planes, no boats. For hours or minutes or days, nothing. In the middle of Bass Strait, time grew as elastic as the water grew monstrous. Beyond our horror, of course, time maintained its more normal constancy. I know now we spent fourteen hours bobbing around in that wild ocean, little more than heads showing above the water. I was wearing a pair of shorts, a T-shirt and a lifejacket.

At some point, I noticed jets roaring overhead. From so far above we would have been like pieces of dandruff on an enraged giant, impossible to find in the roaring white sea. I waved my arms, knowing it was futile, knowing also that to not do so meant something far worse. Later, much later,

I learnt that it was an RAAF squadron of Orions looking for us. All boats in the area that had not headed for safe harbour were also scouring the gale-whipped sea for us.

I could glimpse an island in the distance. Even though the huge waves buffeted me and dragged me and threw me hither and thither, even though my body was senseless with the cold, I kept trying to reach that island. Come what may, I was determined to get there. I succeeded in getting close enough that I could distinguish— when momentarily lifted ahigh on the crest of a wave—beaches.

It was just on nightfall when a fishing boat—and whoever those fishermen were, out in such terrible seas, I am profoundly in their debt—finally found and rescued me. They were five minutes away from abandoning their search. That was luck, and without it I would be dead. I sat in the beautiful warmth of their hold next to a throbbing diesel engine as the fishing boat pitched wildly around me, and cared not about anything. After a long time I finally regained enough of my senses to talk some, and I asked how far away was the island. They looked at me blank-faced, as though I were even madder than they had first supposed. What island? they asked. There is no landfall within bull's roar of here. Only ocean.

Somewhere in that ocean, sometime that night, the fishing boat rendezvoused with a police boat, onto which I was transferred. There was Jim, whom they had rescued shortly before I had been found, some miles away from where the fishing boat had discovered me. Jim came up to me and his eyes were fierce and he said, Where's Fin? We've got to find him. We can't give up.

I am Fin, I said finally, for such was my nickname, but he was already gone, demanding of others the same, while somebody followed him around, trying to calm him, to cover him with blankets, to get him to sit down and rest. I heard him say that I was dead, that I was not dead, that I was. Years later I met one of the policemen who had been on that boat. He said that Jim had been in the final stages of hypothermia and that they had expected him to die.

For many years following our trip, whenever I saw that ocean, I used to shiver and feel frightened and feel myself once more a piece of nothingness lost in vastness, seeing nothing but more ocean and an island that didn't exist. No, that's not exactly how it was, though exactly how it was or who I was I no longer know. People ask, though less now, thank God, what it was like, and sometimes I make up a story or two that I think they want to hear, so they will go away satisfied, and sometimes I say more honestly that I don't know, that it was like staring into the sun for a lifetime and feeling forever blinded, yet forever sensitive to things no one else can apprehend. Then they go away dissatisfied, annoyed at being told what makes no sense, angry at me whom they think somehow touched. Perhaps rightly, perhaps not.

The people who love me never ask me about it. They are easy about it and sense, as I hope I do with them, the big things that one must be easy about with loved ones. For though we are an age obsessed with telling all, it has to be admitted that most of us understand so little that any attempt at telling all is doomed from the outset. We must glean our truths from the few threshings life leaves us.

I do not remember seeing the sea that much, though it was everywhere and I part of it, falling down waves, floundering, having wave after wave crash over me and wondering when I would surface for my next breath. I do remember a feeling, terrible beyond words, that my soul had abandoned my body, and it was not until I met Majda some years later that I felt my soul returning, though not easily, nor without pain. It returned to me like sensation to a terrible wound. I remember vividly a fear so great and so huge and so empty that you would die to avoid it. I remember also my family and friends coming to me as the ocean howled around me (the noise of the wind and the waves, the screaming and screeching, that too was extraordinary), and I wished to continue seeing them and I knew that for that to happen I had to face this fear and not escape it through death, and I wished for death because it was easier than what I was knowing at the time as life.

Majda and I have kids now—three small girls, in fact—and I love them dearly, and when we drive up to visit my brother at Irishtown we come to the point in the road where the land suddenly gives way to the vastness of Bass Strait. A sight wondrous and desolate. A view that jolts. Sometimes one of my girls will say, Did you try and swim that sea, did you, Daddy? and I say, Sort of. Sort of, and they laugh and I laugh, because even to them, more so to them, it is a madness, and it was madness, but I was twenty and Jim was twenty-one and we burnt and we thought we would live forever and we wanted to taunt death, to taste it, and scorn it as only the young feel capable of doing. But it wasn't funny at the time. It wasn't funny for a long, long time afterwards. I didn't laugh for a year or more after it happened. I opened my mouth and raised its corners and made sounds that would be equated with laughter, but nothing was funny. I would lie on the earth like a madman, ear pressed to the ground, and I knew the earth was breathing and me with it, and was forever grateful to know such a thing.

Sometimes one of the girls will say, Was it with Jim? Because they know Jim, he comes to our home occasionally when he is not wandering. He tends to arrive back in Tasmania with the spring winds and leaves not long after the first snowfalls of late autumn. He will stand outside with them, bouncing them on the trampoline for ages, and sometimes we talk, but often we don't have much to say. We save words for others. He laughs with the girls and I like that sound, of his and their laughter rising up through the window from the yard outside. I say, Yes, it was with Jim, but it wasn't really, because some hours after the gale blew up and after our pumps failed and our kayaks sank and we were left simply as two specks adrift in that vast churning ocean, the huge waves swept us apart. I did not see him again, not until after I was rescued. Until then, we each thought that the other was dead and that we might also die. We each felt we were to blame, because we had broken the canoeist's golden rule of always staying together. In that eternity between separation and rescue, we each thought we had killed the other.

If Jim were to read this, he would probably think, no, that is not the way it was, and it isn't, but the way it was and is I don't know. Memory and dreams and childhood visions fuse together to form my poor, confused recollection of that long time, long ago, out there in the middle of Bass Strait. To be honest, I can tell you very little of what took place. I only know that what happened was a mystery, that I did not return from the ocean as the foolhardy young man who had entered it.

I also know that I am no longer a solitary speck in a huge wild ocean. My life is crowded now. I became a writer, but that's not what is so important to me. Sometimes, not very often now, one of our girls finds me alone, crying. And she asks me, Why? I clutch her tight, as if she were a fisherman hauling me out of a wild sea. And I shiver, and I say, I don't know why. I just am.

The Age
19 August 1995

Port Arthur

ONCE UPON A TIME massacres were crimes committed against the people by oppressive regimes: Peterloo, St Petersburg, Amritsar. Horrific as they were, they were events comprehensible as the actions of despotic power seeking to use brutal force to deny people what people wanted as communities and societies: their freedom.

In recent times, in the course of this, the most brutal of centuries, two new ideas arose. One was the notion that if you had a grievance you could vent it through the mass murder of others. Though not a legitimate idea, it is one celebrated and, in a strange way, honoured, increasingly in much popular and high culture. As older notions of community and society gave way to the rise of the notion of us as only an aggregate of consuming individuals, another idea also gained currency: that our enemies are those around us, that the enemy is within. From the Oklahoma bombing to the assassination of Rabin, we now fear our own, and our own fear us.

So the path to Port Arthur was made, littered with the corpses of so many other recent acts of horrendous violence, and the gunman today needed to make no great conceptual or imaginative leap, but seek only to emulate and, one senses in the extraordinary number of deaths, perhaps compete with all his predecessors.

Of course, as Tasmanians we should not have perhaps got so precious about our distance from violence, which was only a momentary hole in both space and time. Tasmania was a society, after all, begat in great violence: against the Aborigines, the convicts and the land itself. Ironically, Port Arthur was the end of the line of an imperial system of terror, the Devil's Island of its day, the greatest of all institutional embodiments of ritualised violence. As a tourist site it has been sanitised, its meanings restricted to the largely superficial: picturesque ruins in the most beautiful, sylvan setting.

Port Arthur will never be the same, a friend said to me, and she was both right and wrong. It won't be the same as it was for many years prior to today, but the gunman's bullets also firmly connect a present and a past world of horrific violence, and only the unravelling of events will tell us how intentional his choice of sites was.

Perhaps we in Tasmania had forgotten what Primo Levi called 'our essential fragility'. We had the vanity to believe we were somehow different, that the currents of change did not wash so far south, to this distant, remote, most beautiful land. We still believed that here a mutual trust held, that we were a people here for others and others for us, and maybe it was never entirely true, but we needed to believe it, for we had little else, and with each year the island went further backwards. On any social or economic indicator Tasmania is the poorest state in Australia and getting poorer. I wonder what will become of us, now that even this myth of our goodness has been taken from us.

As I am writing this, the siege of the gunman continues. Details are few and unreliable, except for the body count, which continues to rise. As of yet, so little is known and yet some things seem clear. We must have strong laws that forbid the ownership of semi-automatic and automatic weapons, and that make the licensing of shooters as stringent as possible, and these laws must be enacted as a matter of the utmost priority. It is wrong to blame what happened on movies or other forms of popular culture. But it is right to ask for a culture that stops being so obsessed with the moment of violence, and instead starts to examine the consequences of violence, and then not simply in terms of physical injury and mutilation, but in the decades and often generations of suffering that ensue. There does seem about the whole horrific affair a dreadful cinematic gloss, from the wisecrack at the door of the restaurant about there being more wasps than Japs, through to the opening killings in that most pulp fictional of settings, the restaurant itself.

It is perhaps not possible to write anything of sense of such a senseless event, a passage of horror that can perhaps never be explained. And yet some sense has to be made of it, or we cannot begin to try to stop such a thing ever happening again. The massacre is only meaningless if we capitulate to its madness as inevitable, as part of the human condition that we must now tolerate.

We need to rediscover that as people we need others not to kill, but to love. And for that we need to rediscover that we are communities. It is possibly a sign of the times that I feel foolish writing such a thing, but it is all I have to offer against what has taken place. My children sleep well, but now I wonder for how long. There are no more once upon times, only nows, and I will have to explain something of this to them. But though I have tried, I cannot answer the insistent question that haunts me and everyone else I know this night as searchers discover yet more and more bodies and the gunman remains at large: How have we come to this?

The Age
29 April 1996

Went for a Swim

NOTHING, WRITES BORGES, is more secondary to
a book's achievement than the intentions of its
author. And in the end novels, the great subversive
medium, subvert not only what society thinks is
right, but what the writer intends to write.

And why?

Because a novel, when it succeeds, takes the
writer beyond his own history and character,
escapes the shackles of his politics and opinions,
and the alchemy of story makes of the writer's soul
that which joins one human being with all human
beings. For this reason Kipling's wonderful stories
can never be reduced to his imperialism, nor Dosto-
evsky's genius invalidated by his anti-Semitism.

Some writers are of course political beings,
others are not, but this is a guide to little. Bad

writers can have admirable politics, while Hamsun and Pound most certainly didn't. Great books can be great campaigning vehicles: one thinks of Turgenev's *A Sportsman's Notebook*, said to have led to the decision to emancipate the serfs, or much of Dickens. Books that are written in opposition to politics, questioning its very basis, can in repressed and tyrannical societies become ironically freighted with enormous political significance: one thinks of *Dr Zhivago* or *Life and Fate* (of the latter it was decreed by the head of the KGB that no one was to read the book for two hundred years).

But Turgenev's or Dickens' political beliefs are no longer why we read these writers, nor is the persecution of Pasternak or the confiscation of Grossman's masterpiece why these books matter. They continue to be read, perhaps, because we recognise them as simply being true to the chaos of life. If a novel can achieve this, it can never be reduced to an ideology, and will always remain the enemy of lies and oppression.

Writing does not excuse a writer from political choices and actions, but nor does it demand them of him. These are matters between a man and a soul, which a writer must face up to along with the plumber, the hairdresser and the executive. Paradoxically, the writers most concerned about making politics part of their work often write work that is autistic to the politics of its times; while writers with almost no interest sometimes write most perceptively of their era: amidst the agitprop wastes of the 1920s, no one more shrewdly foretold the political apocalypse looming than Kafka, the man who recorded the most historically signifi- cant event in his life, the start of World War I, with a fine sense of human proportion: 'Morning: war declared. Afternoon: went for a swim.'

There are so many forces in the world that divide us deeply and murderously. In recent times we have lived through not so much a crisis of politics as a collapse of that most human attribute, empathy—a collapse so catastrophic it sometimes appears to be a crisis of love, manifest in epidemics of loneliness and depression. This strange event seems most pronounced in the West in the USA, a country where pessimism about the future of the novel has become its most persistent literary tradition.

We cannot escape politics, history, religion, nationalism—for their sources lie as deep in our hearts as love and goodness, perhaps even deeper. But at its best, art reminds us of all that we share, of all that brings us together.

For this reason books matter. For this reason books aren't just novelty items or celebrity front- list accompaniments; one more marketing platform for the famous and the powerful. In a world where the road to the new tyrannies is paved with the fear of others, great books show us that we are neither alone, nor in the end that different; that what joins us is always more important than what divides us; and that the price of division is ever the obscenity of oppression.

Bookforum
May 2008

Self-massaging Ugg Boots

WRITERS, STALIN FAMOUSLY DECLARED, were engineers of the human soul. This old idea seems sadly renascent. Recently I read that 'culture is the software of the nation'.

Yet great art is the soul, not its maker, far less its engineer or software, and it reminds us of the chaos in every human heart. In their greatest moments, artists and the art they make exist in opposition, speaking to those things that we need as individuals but that seemingly threaten us as societies: truth, freedom, non-conformity, desire, and so on.

All great art is amoral. It offers neither guidance on how to live, nor wisdom on how to reconcile with this world. It simply takes us into the chaotic soul of things, reminding us of the full possibilities of this life.

Art is the closest thing we have to holding on to that inner spirit world that we feel always to be on the verge of vanishing and that we recall only as the vaguest of sensations: the touch of a loved one, the shadow of a forgotten tree, the sound of a parent crying.

And yet there can be no doubt that art influences politics and history, a fact the most powerful readily acknowledge. 'Do you know,' Napoleon once said to Fontanes, 'what fills me most with wonder? The powerlessness of force to establish anything. There are only two powers in the world: the sword and the mind. In the end the sword is always conquered by the mind.'

It is obvious that art is also a series of products subject to fashion and commerce. But it is not reducible to a product in the way self-massaging ugg boots I saw for sale in Harvey Norman are.

Art is, of course, a guarantee of nothing. Nor is love. But for similar reasons we have not yet discovered a way of living without it. Unlike self-massaging ugg boots, we need it.

'In reading the gospels,' wrote Oscar Wilde when in Reading Gaol—and let us not forget that there he was allowed nothing else to read—'I see the continual assertion of the imagination as the basis of all spiritual and material life. I see also that to Christ imagination was simply a form of love.'

This seems a beautiful, and a very true, observation. We live in a world where it is relentlessly and arrogantly presumed that all is knowable and sayable; that everything can be encapsulated in some formula of words.

Worse, we feel that unless we can measure something as material worth or tangible power, it is irrelevant.

And yet all of life that matters happens in a realm beyond knowing and measuring, and nothing is more unsayable, unknowable, immeasurable, more isolated from analysis than acts of the imagination fired by love.

Sadly, we in Australia have in recent years become largely indifferent, even sometimes hostile, to such acts. There has developed a shame about our national experience and those artists who seek to speak to it, not so distant from the colonial cringe of the 1950s.

We need change. We could once more as a nation commit to the idea of art, but not as a national fashion accessory in the manner of a 1980s ALP policy platform nor, as was argued the following decade, of art as an economic driver. For while art can be harnessed to such uses, it is not why it matters.

We could decide to acknowledge and honour art as central to what we are as human beings. Because to fail to recognise its centrality to our humanity is to leave the realms of civil society and public life caught in a coarsening of public rhetoric and collapse of empathy that has been wrong, inhumane and ultimately damaging to us as a people.

Of course, we won't.

But it is worth thinking about, if only because art is knowing ourselves more fully as human beings and, more than ever, we need that knowledge at the centre of what we now do. And yet, more than ever, it is absent. The empire's prefects and satraps take counsel only from the abacus, call on the flagellator to restore order, and cannot understand why the barbarians are advancing. Without art, without an honouring of its foundation in love, there is no answer that can be made to the scream of the child whose mother was just blown up in yet one more Baghdad bomb blast, or the silence of the Bangladeshi peasant watching his home and village disappearing beneath a rising sea.

The Sydney Morning Herald
15 January 2008

It's Peter Dom

In this world
we walk on the roof of hell
gazing at flowers
Issa

In March 1996, just before setting out on a
solo trip to walk the rugged Western Arthurs in
Tasmania's south-west, Peter Dombrovskis called.
He wanted to talk about a forthcoming book of
his photographs of Mount Wellington for which I
was writing an introductory essay. The mountain
defines Hobart and links it to the great wildlands
of Tasmania. For generations Hobartians have
walked, climbed, camped, tobogganed, swum and
played over the mountain. Peter worried that the
growing emphasis on notions of 'sacred wilderness'

created a lie, or rather that it was the other pole of a lie. He lived on one of the mountain's higher flanks, and for him the mountain showed that the natural world wasn't something separate from human beings but the essence of us.

Peter talked of doing a book on gardens to further explore this idea. In a world in which humanity is ever more autistic to the natural world, he felt that anything that allowed people communion with nature mattered. Looking back on it now, I think he found all ways of being part of nature at once rich and mysterious. Rather than being dogmatic, Peter was curious.

He asked me about the boulders on the upper Huon River. He knew I was one of the few who had kayaked it and he wanted to know what they were like.

Why? I asked.

Because Olegas told me that they were beautiful, he said. One day I'd like to photograph them.

Olegas was Olegas Truchanas, a Lithuanian who arrived in Tasmania post-World War II and established a considerable reputation as both an explorer and landscape photographer. Truchanas had been the first to kayak the upper Huon, as well as the Gordon River. In one of several ironies, he worked as a draftsman for Tasmania's Hydro-Electric Commission, which, with its dams, was systematically destroying the wildlands that Truchanas was exploring, photographing and fighting to protect.

In the 1960s Truchanas began staging slide shows in the Hobart City Hall, showing the threatened wildlands with accompanying classical music. From the beginning these seemingly innocuous couplings of image and music were understood as the most political of events.

Then, in the great bushfire of 1967, his home and with it his slide collection was lost. Truchanas, now ageing, returned to the south-west to try to rebuild his archive of images of all that was on the verge of vanishing. In 1972, on a kayaking trip down the now threatened Gordon River, he lost his footing on a submerged log and disappeared into the dark, tannin-stained waters.

'He had been destroyed, with Biblical simplicity,' wrote Truchanas' friend Max Angus, 'by two of the elements, fire and water. Five years had passed between their brief and terrible visits. He had perished in the river he sought to save. Classical mythology affords no stronger example of the drama of the incorruptible man who passes into legend.'

It was a young man who three days later found Truchanas' drowned body. He was the fatherless son of a Latvian migrant, born in a refugee camp in Germany in 1945, for whom Olegas had become a father-figure, teaching him canoeing and photography. His name was Peter Dombrovskis.

A month later Dombrovskis returned to Lake Pedder, which Truchanas through his kayaking trip had been attempting to help save. From the same spot on the Coronets where Truchanas once had taken a photograph, he took an almost identical picture of the lake and its famed beach.

'I like to think,' Dombrovskis later said, 'I'm carrying on where Olegas left off, in my own way, finishing the work he started.'

But Lake Pedder was as doomed as Truchanas. Within three years it would vanish.

Yet Truchanas' influence soared in the 1970s and 1980s, spurred on by the publication of a book of his photographs, *The World of Olegas Truchanas* (1975). As the environmental movement went mainstream, Truchanas passed into myth as a martyr. Meanwhile, with the publication of Dombrovskis' early books *The Quiet Land* (1977) and *Wild Rivers* (1983) and his bestselling wilderness calendars, he became seen as Truchanas' heir. His photograph of the Franklin River at Rock Island Bend became the most celebrated landscape photograph in Australian history. Used by conservationists, it was said to have helped sway the federal election of 1983 in favour of Bob Hawke's Australian Labor Party which promised to save the Franklin River.

It is perhaps not possible to convey what powerful effect the example of Olegas Truchanas and Peter Dombrovskis—the artist as adventurer; the merging of life and art; the radical and liberating possibilities of the natural world—had upon many Tasmanians growing up in the benighted, marginal and often self-hating Tasmania of the 1970s and 1980s. They created another Tasmania; an invitation to dream open to all.

Outside of Tasmania, the work of Truchanas and Dombrovskis has often appeared baffling. To some, their representations of landscape seem at best conventional, drawing from a romantic tradition that seems outdated, even reactionary. That their work has endured is strange; that it had radical political edge even more mysterious, and in some ways reprehensible. For the antipathy to art and artists in Australia that remains such a strong and destructive force in our national life sometimes appears to have been internalised and taken up by the Australian art world itself. It expresses itself variously: that great Australian lack of generosity to difference as well as a fear of any art that has political connotation, or, for that matter, spirit. It has also led to a culture of the corral: unless an artist is on the inside, part of a grant and gallery and critic system, they are not an artist.

Truchanas was a draftsman. Dombrovskis made a journeyman living, selling his images as postcards, calendars and books. They lived in Tasmania and made art about Tasmania, an island at once alien and marginal to Australia. It's hard to imagine artists more on the outside.

To the extent they had a politics, it was not the monocultural nationalism of the Labor Party that had so often been the bedrock creed for how Australian art was divined. Since Federation, Australian art was seen to have a mission to make a single national culture in the image of either its great coastal cities or its mainland dry outback. Whatever the aesthetic it wore as its motley, that was the goal.

Though a nation, Australia is not one country but many, and one of these is the country of Tasmania. Both men created an idea of Tasmania that could not be dismissed as regional or small, and that, like all powerful artistic ideas, contained a universe within it. For many on the island, these two artists were liberating—they showed us we lived not imprisoned in a small place dully conformist to a weary, century-old trope, but as part of a world of infinite possibility. But in so doing they also drew attention to the profound human choice that went with that world. To seek to know it better, to love it, or to agree to its destruction.

Talent is love, Tolstoy once said. The idea that great art is made out of love and can only be comprehended through love recurs through history in defiance of schools, traditions, aesthetics and ideologies. Love unleavened, of course, leads to kitsch. But with the yeast of circumstance, history and ambition added, enduring work sometimes arises.

Dombrovskis' work has been criticised as determinedly false, refusing to acknowledge the human element of the natural world by rarely showing humans or human artefacts. But the argument seems to make no more sense than applying it to abstract art. Dombrovskis spoke of how a photograph had to be filled with the character of the photographer or it was nothing. His images are, finally, an idea of humanity. But it is a particular and haunting idea of who we are and what we might be.

It is true that the conservation movement of the 1980s promoted a sense of 'wilderness' in which man had never been and should never intrude upon. Given human history in Tasmania is at least 40,000 years old and man has played a key role in shaping these wildlands for that long, such an idea was both demonstrably untrue and, as Dombrovskis understood, damaging to our souls. Though both men were environmentalists, and though that same movement used their images to promote environmental causes, as the years pass, as the politics recede, the images endure and seem to speak of something much larger and more evocative than the battles of that era. Much of Dombrovskis' later work finds erotic images of women in abstracted landscapes. The close-up still lifes of kelp-wrack, broken sea shells, myrtle leaf swirls, sand rib, snow-gum bark and river spume grow ever more mysterious, open and powerful.

I sometimes think both Truchanas' and Dombrovskis' attitude to the natural world of Tasmania can only be understood as a response to the immense human horror of World War II in Eastern Europe. At the edge of the world, where the contours of progress were more visible than at its centre, two photographers, refugees of the last great global conflict of nation and ideology against nation and ideology, perhaps came closer than many of their more celebrated peers in speaking of the conflict to come—of man against the natural world, and the terrible cost not just to our environment and economy, but to our humanity if we did not try to prevent it, if we did not try to understand ourselves and our world differently.

The storyteller, writes Walter Benjamin, is the man who would let the flame of his story consume the wick of his life. Peter was precise about language, and he may have dismissed such an idea. Certainly he would have seen no relevance to himself. But sometimes there is about an artist's life a profound and terrible poetry.

The Monday following my phone call with Peter I was driving to Salamanca through black clouds and heavy-dropped rain that sweeps and slaps rather than falls, while Hobart's higher suburbs were being coated in snow. The radio news said a solo walker had failed to return from a walking trip to the Western Arthurs. I rang a friend who worked in police search and rescue.

It's Peter Dom, he said.

They searched in blizzards for three days. Far below, floodwaters rose and covered the beautiful boulders of the upper Huon River. They found him kneeling, looking out to the south-west wild-lands. He had been dead for some days, killed by a massive heart attack. As the weather was about to change, Peter had fallen to his knees, bowing before the world he had invited us to love and discover ourselves anew in.

Art & Australia
Spring 2010

The Unbearable Lightness of Borges

In 1960, SIX EMINENT PUBLISHERS from six different countries met and established a new prize, the
Prix Formentor, to which they attached a large
purse, and the promise of publication in each of
the six different countries for the winner.

The first prize in 1961 was shared by Samuel
Beckett and an aged, blind librarian from Buenos
Aires, little known even in his own country. His
name was Jorge Luis Borges.

'Fame is a form of incomprehension, perhaps
the worst,' Borges had written two decades earlier
when he was a struggling, shy and almost entirely
unknown Argentinian writer. Yet, propelled by
the Prix Formentor, fame was now to be his fate,

and he accepted it with grace. By the end of the decade Mick Jagger, ever a barometer of fashion, reclined in a bath in Nicholas Roeg's film *Performance*, reading Borges' *Ficciones*.

Borges arrived internationally at a moment when literature seemed spent. The writings of the time were weighed down by a stifling naturalism on one hand, and on the other by a sclerotic modernist experiment so deadening that the books failed to either sell or be read. Writing's great modernists—Hamsen, Joyce, Kafka, Mann, Joseph Roth—were either dead or so advanced in their creative infirmity—Dos Passos, Faulkner, Hemingway all come to mind—that many wished them so; literature's chief promotional device, the Nobel Prize, seemed to be sinking into an irrelevant decrepitude. Film and television, rather than novels, threatened to become the natural media for storytelling.

Literature had lost its audience, its irreverence, its capacity for games, for invention: in short, both its authority and capacity as a creative force. As though they were gifts he was bestowing, Borges, ever a generous man, gave all these virtues and more back to the world of letters.

In the course of the next twenty years literature was to be reinvented as an artistic and popular force by other South American writers. The innovative, often astonishing works of Márquez,

Neruda, Fuentes, Amado, Infante, Ribeiro, Puig, Carpentier, Cortázar and Vargas Llosa found widespread international favour, and influenced writers everywhere. This miraculous alchemy was heralded by the blind librarian of Buenos Aires whose sparely written stories returned fiction to storytelling, whose vertiginous tales of tigers, labyrinths, gauchos and bandits were fun, subversive, amusing, and yet managed, in Kafka's memorable phrase, to be the axe that smashes the frozen sea within.

Born in Argentina in 1899, a country rent by rival nationalisms, Borges early on broke with the fashionable mission of nationalist letters that elevated novels full of local incident and colour, as well as rejecting their opponents, the international modernists, who despised all things local as regional, and therefore (here the danger of pejorative synonyms being mistaken for truths) mediocre.

Borges—and in this there is much for our often still puerile literati to learn—held that distance from Europe allowed a writer to reinterpret the Western literary tradition. For Borges distance was a liberating virtue, not an oppressive tyranny. This did not mean that a writer need be limited 'to purely Argentine subjects in order to be Argentine'. 'Our patrimony is the universe,' he argued. 'We should essay all themes.' A writer who acted within that Western literary tradition, but who, at the same time, did not feel tied to it by any special devotion, was capable of an irreverence that made innovation possible. Borges' position was that of the outsider: devoted neither to literary nor national tradition, but profoundly shaped by both, and accordingly capable of an irreverence that made innovation possible.

In his youth he wrote poems in praise of the Bolshevik Revolution, but his politics later altered to a polite form of anarchism: he hoped for a society that had no need for government. He was strongly opposed to Peronism, and for his troubles was made Buenos Aires' official inspector of poultry in 1946. In his old age he sided with the military junta that ran his country, though what he meant by this was ambiguous: 'I am a member of the Conservative Party,' he wrote in 1970, 'which is in itself a form of scepticism.'

In any case, as he observed of Kipling, a great writer succeeds in spite of his beliefs, because their work transcends its own often narrow concerns. He believed with Plato that writers are 'the scribes of a god who moves them against their own will, against their intentions, just as a magnet moves a series of iron rings'. He was opposed to the then fashionable Sartrean notion of the committed writer; like Kipling, his politics obscured his achievements, and many believed his accommodation of the Argentinian generals cost him the Nobel Prize.

Traumatised by having sex introduced to him by his father's whore, he lived with his mother in Buenos Aires until her death when he was in his seventies. He had a great affection for women, but for much of his life little luck. He was seen with many, often beautiful, women, contracted one unsuccessful and, at the end of his life, one successful marriage. Following psychoanalysis for his impotence in the mid-1940s he had one of his two main creative outbursts, in which period he wrote the short stories that make up his great book *El-Aleph*. The obvious assumption of cause and effect here is not necessarily the right conclusion to draw. Time, as Borges was highly aware, is successive, but the workings of the springs and coils of the soul are not.

Unlike many of the South Americans who followed in his wake, in what became known as the Boom, Borges was not an exponent of the Baroque, a style he had discarded as a youthful excess. Nor was his work rooted in what the Cuban Alejo Carpentier first famously described in 1949 as 'lo real maravilloso' (literally: 'the real marvellous'), and which later became popularised as the 'magical realism' of the everyday Latin American world.

Borges was a classicist in style. By his own

admission he grew up in a library of English books, and his works seemed more rooted in an ethereal erudition than in the eroticised earthiness of a Márquez or an Amado. Borges rightly described his own progress as that 'from the mythologies of the slums and the outskirts of the city to games with time and infinity'. His was, as a biographer, James Woodall, has written, 'a new metaphysical daring in fiction'.

He never wrote a novel, though his work, in its concerns, its clarity and its innovation, carries the weight and authority of that of the very greatest of novelists. 'It is a laborious madness and an impoverishing one, the madness of composing vast books,' wrote Borges, 'setting out in 500 pages an idea that can be perfectly related orally in five minutes. The better way to go about it is to pretend that those books already exist, and offer a summary, a commentary on them . . . I have chosen to write notes on imaginary books.' And in so doing, he suggested in a few pages worlds of vast mystery and wonder.

Unlike Márquez and the magical realists, who looked so much to the North Americans—most particularly Faulkner, whom they in their youth called the Old Man, the Colonel who remained forever at the centre of their literary labyrinths— Borges, for all his breadth of reading, looked to European, and specifically English writing. The modernist writer par excellence, his influences were however anything but fashionable modernists.

Chesterton, Stevenson, Kipling, Thomas de Quincey were his masters, yet as he once pointed out, a writer invents his own influences as surely as his own work: to reread any of these writers after reading Borges is to discover depths and nuances of meaning that hitherto were invisible. But then, as Borges also wrote, reading is ultimately a more profound, more intellectual and more creative act than writing. His works were in many ways written as homage to the act of reading. They also serve as a reawakening for the reader to the mysterious profundity of that act of grace, the moment when a reader grants the written word the authority of their life and soul.

The English, as opposed to the Hispanic, character of the writers he favoured was not an accidental choice. Borges had inherited from his English grandmother, Fanny Haslam, a condition that saw the retinas of his eyes slowly detach, and a belief in his own Englishness, which he understood as a sort of separateness and perhaps a solace for his shyness. Equally fluent from an early age in Spanish and English (in consequence of his Northumbrian grandmother he spoke the latter with a slight Northern cast), translating Oscar Wilde's *The Happy Prince* into Spanish at the age of nine, Borges developed the highest regard for English as a language of literature. Correspondingly, his first and principal understanding of literature was of it as English writing, leading him to first read even the greatest work of his own literature—*Don Quixote*—in English translation. The *Quixote*, Borges later noted, 'was first and foremost a pleasant book; it is now an occasion for patriotic toasts, grammatical arrogance, obscene deluxe editions'.

In *Collected Fictions: Jorge Luis Borges* (1999), a deluxe edition of Borges' stories newly translated by Andrew Hurley, we have the beginnings of a similar incomprehension born of an over-reverence, unhappily coupled to a desire for a Borges canon that most benefits his estate, rather than his readers, or his writing as he wrote it.

The book's redeeming virtue—and it is considerable—lies in its organisation of Borges' principal stories in the order they were published originally, rather than in the confused compendiums that have served the English-speaking world for so long. By virtue of its breadth and this organisation, it is the best introduction to Borges in our language, and for that reason an important work. One can only add that this is perhaps more in the nature of an indictment than a recommendation.

Its vice lies in its translations. It is not that these are bad: it is just that we already have better. Hurley's translations, though not markedly different from those of his often illustrious predecessors, such as Alastair Reid, tend, where they differ, to be inferior. But that is only part of the problem.

There is little wrong with these translations when compared to their predecessors, because there is little different. But what differences there are tend to be for the worse rather than the better. Where Borges' stories were light, irreverent and often very funny, this compendium in its entirety takes on the portentous weight and feel of an American novel written by one of the masters of that empire in its terminal infirmity, whereby a book's significance seems directly connected to its heaviness. Borges' stories never weighed anything.

This was never more evident than with the best translations of all: those made of much of his work by Borges himself, in collaboration with the North American Norman Thomas di Giovanni. Introducing one of his own translations, Borges wrote that Spanish and English 'are not, as is often taken for granted, a set of interchangeable synonyms but are two possible ways of viewing and ordering reality'. Accordingly, his aim was always to make 'the text read as though it had been written in English', an admirable virtue not always apparent in some of Hurley's uneasier translations.

Borges, better read in English than most English, seemed to see his translations as being as much an original work as the Spanish stories

with which they shared the same tales and
characters. Where Hurley's Borges sometimes
becomes wordy, muddy, or overly ornate, Borges'
Borges is crystal clear, punchy, and well told. It
will be to our loss if these great works written
in English by Borges disappear from publishers'
lists and hence our culture in the wake of this
official translation.

It does then seem an oddity—and a destructive
one at that—for us to be presented with a book
that has freshly translated from the Spanish many
stories for which we already have translations
done by Borges himself.

'Nothing is as co-substantial with literature
and its modest mystery,' Borges once commented,
'as the questions raised by translation.' The
inescapable question raised here is why translate
from the Spanish when we already have originals
written by Borges in our language?

The answer would seem to lie in a brief note
at the end of *Collected Fictions*, which tells us that
Borges' literary estate—the Borges Foundation—
specified that all the translations in this volume
be made from the Spanish collected works. It is
not possible to say whether this direction was for
literary reasons, or whether it was the deadening
hand of a literary estate keeping copyright in its
own control by neatly leapfrogging—and hence
avoiding—the generous arrangement made by

Borges that saw copyright and royalties half-owned by his collaborator, di Giovanni.

Maybe none of this matters. Borges was finally sanguine about translation and so perhaps should we be. 'Each language is a tradition, each word a shared symbol,' wrote Borges. 'The changes that an innovator may make are trifling.' One imagines him revelling in the Borgesian confusions of multiple translations.

His contempt for authorised, definitive translations (which he thought the property of ideology and religion, but not letters) was perhaps partly coupled to his humility. Borges never succumbed to what he believed to be 'the basest of art's temptations: the temptation to be a genius'. He constantly deflated any estimation of his own work beyond that of storytelling, and even in this regard he felt, somewhat similarly to William Morris, that he only discovered, rather than invented stories. It also arose—one guesses—from his lively awareness of the infinite openness of literature, of the labyrinthine nature of stories, which each writer and each translator partly stripped away, and partly added to. 'There is no intellectual exercise,' concluded Borges, 'that is not ultimately futile.'

Such scepticism about life, about thought, about the fictional nature of all things informed his games 'with time and infinity'. He regarded scholarship as a branch of fabulous literature, and fabulous literature as a way of approaching the truth. His work consequently blurred boundaries: essays read like stories and vice versa. His short story 'Pierre Menard: Author of the Quixote' has been described by eminent anthologist Ilan Stavans as 'probably the most influential essay ever written in Latin America'.

His influence on those writers who have succeeded him seems as protean as his sources: from Julio Cortázar's seminal novel *Hopscotch*, inspired by the Borges story 'The Garden of Forking Paths'; to Gabriel García Márquez's *One Hundred Years of Solitude*, which combined the influence of Pablo Neruda's sensual earthiness with Borgesian concerns as to the way reality is endlessly fictional, and fictions are endlessly realistic; to Salman Rushdie, whose recent and far less inspiring *The Ground Beneath Her Feet* reads like a bad elaboration of a Borges story, an uncomfortable conclusion not helped by the numerous knowing references made through the novel both to Borges' stories and tropes.

The epitaph 'a writer's writer' seems unfair to one so pleasurable to read, yet inevitable for a writer with such an extraordinary—the adjective is for once justified—capacity to represent a complex world in a few sentences; for whom everything in the world might be the seed of a possible heaven—or a possible hell: 'a face, a word, a compass, an advertisement'.

His joy in language, both his own and others, was immense: visiting Deerhurst Saxon church in the Cotswolds in 1963, he recited in Old English the Lord's Prayer. His sentences were beautifully sculpted, never dull, and often short stories in themselves. In 'Tlön, Uqbar, Orbis Tertius' we find the following: 'My father had forged one of those close English friendships with him (the first adjective is perhaps excessive) that begin by excluding confidences and end by eliminating conversation.'

His method was to narrate 'events as though I didn't fully understand them', furthering his sense that 'literature is naught but guided dreaming'. His tools were irony, and a disingenuous sense of humour that cloaked a darker sensibility. Bioy Casares recalled an early idea of Borges' for a story, never written, about a Dr Praetorious: 'a large, easygoing German school principal who, by using annoying means (obligatory games, never-ending music), would torture and kill young children'.

Borges claimed he wished to write 'plain tales' that entertained and touched people. 'I dare not say they are simple, there is not a simple page, a simple word on earth—for all pages, all words, predicate the universe, whose most notorious attribute is its complexity.'

Confucius and Wilkie Collins, the Kabbalah and Kipling, Lao Tzu and Martín Fierro all seem to come together effortlessly in Borges' strange tales. Borges could indirectly satirise his own style of writing in stories such as 'The Approach to Al-Mu'tasim', in which a Bombay attorney takes to writing detective novels that display 'the dual, and implausible influence of Wilkie Collins and the illustrious twelfth-century Persian poet Farid al-Din Attar'. Mystical undercurrents and detective-novel plots, gaucho knife fights and the problem of eternal return, a scholar given the gift of Shakespeare's memory, which becomes for him an utter torment; Chinese women pirates and fantastic invented second worlds that begin to intrude on the real world and then overtake it, a Czech Jewish writer who beseeches God for time to write his great book, and composes it in its entirety, word for word, in the instant before he is shot dead by a German firing squad; a man who can remember everything that ever happened: on and on the extraordinary conceits flow.

His work laid little claim to the psychological: in this it marked a singular rupture with the tradition begun so spectacularly by Flaubert a century before. Above all else, Borges belonged, believed Bioy Casares, to that 'tradition of the great novelists and short story writers, that is, the tradition of the storytellers'. When he and Borges would meet, wrote Bioy Casares, Borges 'usually declares that he has some news about one character or another; as if he had just seen them, or had been living with them; he tells me what Frogman or Montenegro had been doing the day before, or what Bonavena or Mrs Ruiz Villalba had said'.

His was a joy in life and a joy in stories, two virtues not commonly associated with literature. 'I hope the reader may find in my pages something that merits being remembered,' Borges wrote in a foreword to one of his later works. 'In this world, beauty is so common.'

His work opened up Borges to the charges of what Bioy Casares called 'the habitual conflict between books and life'. In his own soul, one suspects there was no such conflict. Finally the world and the word became one, Borges' universe became Borges the world-famous writer. 'A man sets himself the task of drawing the world,' he wrote in old age. 'As the years pass, he fills the empty space with images of provinces and kingdoms, mountains, bays, ships, islands, fish, houses, instruments, stars, horses and people. Just before he dies, he discovers that the patient labyrinth of lines traces the image of his own face.'

In 'Parable of the Palace', the Yellow Emperor's poet is put to death for capturing the totality of the marvel and the enormity of his great palace in a single poem. But such legends, concludes Borges, 'are simply literary fictions . . . and his [the poet's] descendants still seek, though they shall never find, the word for the universe'. Similarly it is impossible to find a word that might describe Borges' stories. Beauty may be common, but writing of such wonder is not.

The Age
19 June 1999

Caramba

Franz Kafka's friendship with Max Brod, wrote Walter Benjamin, 'is a question mark which he chose to put in the margin of his life'.

In the annals of twentieth-century literature, Jorge Luis Borges' friendship with his English translator, Norman Thomas di Giovanni, may rank, on the evidence of di Giovanni's book (*The Lesson of the Master: On Borges and his Work*, 2003), as no less perplexing.

Recounting through eight essays discussing aspects of Borges and his work the years he spent with the great Argentinian writer, di Giovanni's prose can sometimes seem as leaden and dull as Borges was otherwise. Yet between 1967 and 1972, in collaboration with di Giovanni, Borges—blind, old and fearful of his powers fading—reworked some of his best stories and poems into what are arguably not fine translations of the greatest Spanish-language writer of the twentieth century, but some of twentieth-century English literature's finest original works.

To his credit di Giovanni makes no claim for himself other than his friendship and work with Borges, and his book is, by its own admission, a modest volume that seeks to be, and succeeds as, an act of homage to Borges, the man he acknowledges as his master.

Sometimes melancholic and occasionally irritable, the book's touchstone is di Giovanni's friendship with Borges and the insights that provides. Though di Giovanni is discreet and respectful, the book offers up the occasional fascinating tidbit. On Borges' various, hapless passions for Buenos Aires society women with literary pretensions, di Giovanni notes that Borges described them to him as 'all unforgettable, all forgotten'. The forewords Borges wrote for their books, were, 'it was said, the kiss of death' in Argentinian literary circles.

These essays, possibly not in spite of but because of di Giovanni's occasional meandering and pedantry, reveal Borges as a very human figure, an idea of the writer at odds with the monstrous literary genius he is too often lauded as. Di Giovanni despises such over-reverence of

Borges, both because of its untruth and the way such a view corrupts readings and translations of a writer he views as a great storyteller.

Borges himself translated from English into Spanish, and his translations would seem to speak to his own conception of the great artistic possibilities of translation. For example, William Faulkner's pivotal influence on the writers of the Latin American Boom has been acknowledged by everyone from Gabriel García Márquez to Maria Vargas Llosa. But it was not the Faulkner of *As I Lay Dying* and *The Sound and the Fury* that initially fired these writers, but, above all else, the Faulkner of *The Wild Palms*, as rendered in Spanish by Borges. Could Borges' translation of *The Wild Palms* be the work of genius the original is not; the great novel he, Borges, never wrote?

For all his belief in the creative possibilities in translating, Borges was highly aware of the level of incompetence and misunderstanding that can attend translation.

He once read an English translation of a Chinese philosopher containing the following passage: 'A man condemned to death doesn't care that he is standing at the edge of a precipice, for he has already renounced life.' This was attended by a footnote by the translator arguing for the superiority of this translation over that made by a rival Sinologist, which read: 'The servants destroy the works of art, and they will have to judge their beauties and defects.'

At that moment, wrote Borges, 'a mysterious scepticism slipped into my soul'.

But such scepticism did not incline Borges toward the fashion for literal translations, which, he argued in a lecture at Harvard in 1967, 'would have been a crime to translators in ages past. They were thinking of something far worthier. They wanted to prove that the vernacular was as capable of a great poem as the original.'

Among his audience was the young American translator Norman Thomas di Giovanni. He wrote to Borges, asking to meet. Curiously, Borges, notorious for never answering letters, replied.

Di Giovanni met not the great Borges but an old man: shy, lacking in confidence, depressed with his recent marriage and fearful that he had lost his ability to write, so unable to effect a change in his life that di Giovanni was later to engineer a trip to Cordoba to facilitate Borges' divorce from his second wife, Elsa Astete Millán.

Together, they sought to honour Borges' glorious vision of what was possible with translation: work as good as, even better than, the original. To translate, for Borges, was an invitation to create no less significant than the invitation to write.

Translators tend to be poorly paid and overworked. Though some gain an acquaintanceship, and occasionally a friendship, with a writer, this is rare. They of necessity must do their work quickly, generally in a different country, and their contact with an author is normally restricted to a brief correspondence in which a few factual questions about local detail are asked and answered.

The collaboration of di Giovanni and Borges was of a different order. They quickly hit on a process not so much of translation as, in Borges' words, 're-creation' of his works in English.

Daily they would meet in the gloomy recesses of the National Library of Argentina, where Borges enjoyed a sinecure as director. Here they revelled in books and words, di Giovanni recalling how they would both savour smelling an ancient dictionary of the Spanish Royal Academy that sat on the table on which they worked, discussing nuances of meaning and purpose, sometimes introducing or deleting whole sentences, or even paragraphs, always attempting to ensure that the overall story was enhanced in its English incarnation.

At such work, wrote Borges, they didn't consider themselves two men: 'We think we are really one mind at work.' Pedantic as they were, their bedrock was ideas and story, not words, acting on Borges' belief that he tried 'to say what I have to say perhaps not through words, but in spite of them'. Paradoxically, though their grail was not style, their 're-creations' contain English of beauty, and sometimes dazzling virtuosity.

Borges brought to the task several unusual qualities. He was bilingual, having grown up, as he put it, 'in a garden, behind a fence of iron palings, and in a library of endless English books'. As an adult he would often conceive titles, phrases and sentences for his works in English and then translate them back into Spanish.

For all his ambition with his English stories, Borges' ultimate position on translating was sanguine: he believed the test of great literature was precisely its capacity to survive mistranslation and remain compelling.

'The "perfect" page is precisely the one that consists of those delicate fringes that are so easily worn away,' wrote Borges. 'On the contrary, the page that becomes immortal can traverse the fires of typographical errors, approximate translations, and inattentive or erroneous readings without losing its soul in the process . . . *Don Quixote* wins posthumous battles against his translators and survives each and every careless version . . . the writer's overriding passion is his subject . . . Genuine literature is as indifferent to a rough hewn phrase as it is to a smooth sentence.'

Di Giovanni lacks such largeness. He nitpicks at the failings of other more recent translations;

notably Andrew Hurley's much vaunted 1998 compendium of Borges' fiction. His real criticism is never made; it is more, one suspects, in the nature of the deepest of personal hurts.

Such carping particularly and di Giovanni's book generally makes little sense without understanding his own cruel fate at the hands of the Borges Estate, administered by Borges' third, last wife of fewer than two months, Maria Kodama.

Translators are normally either paid a set, small fee by the publisher for their work, or, less commonly, a very low percentage of royalties. Borges had hit on a characteristically generous and highly unusual agreement with di Giovanni that saw them split royalties equally. For the Borges Estate, Borges' arrangement meant a 50 per cent reduction in its income from English language editions of some of Borges' major works.

In the mid-1990s Maria Kodama had a New York agent negotiate a lucrative new English language deal, selling the English translation rights to Borges' complete Spanish works. Henceforth, these would be the basis of the official English language editions, authorised by Borges' own estate, rendering, at a stroke, Borges and di Giovanni's work redundant and unpublishable, and giving Maria Kodama full copyright and the Borges Estate 100 per cent of English royalties. Bizarrely, in the name of Borges, this was condemning to obscurity those very works Borges had co-authored in English.

Di Giovanni's story, which is implicit but never told in this odd volume, is one of a loyal friend whose most significant work has been largely lost, hopefully not permanently, because of the woman Borges loved expressing her ongoing respect for her dead husband by managing his literary estate with a strong hand. Literature does not lend itself to the pathos of such a story, because love always plays better between the clapboards than friendship.

Perhaps this is why, finally, we recognise Borges less in di Giovanni's pages than we do in Borges' own, and why we feel we come closest to Borges in his own writings when he speaks of his love for other writers' books: not in such works' triumph over death, but in their transcendence of the individual soul. As Borges had Shakespeare write, and di Giovanni translate: 'I, who have been no man, am all men.'

All collaboration is mysterious, wrote Borges. On di Giovanni reading him the finished English draft of his feted story 'The Circular Ruins', Borges wept.

'Caramba,' said Borges. 'I wish I could still write like that.'

Yet through his friendship with Norman Thomas di Giovanni, no longer in Spanish but in the tongue of his Staffordshire grandmother, in the language of the writers he revered, Shakespeare and Stevenson and de Quincey and Chesterton, Borges still was writing like that.

Like the ironies in which he delighted, Borges' tears, unexpected as they are beautiful, appear to us as a truth pregnant with a destiny that once realised, would, through the actions of his widow, finally prove unfulfilled.

But then, as Borges, so often disappointed and humiliated in love, had told di Giovanni on his first morning in Buenos Aires, 'Here, in Argentina, friendship is more important than love.'

The Age
12 July 2003

Nelson Algren's War with America

NELSON ALGREN'S LIFE is terrifying in its proof that talent, love and a determination to speak truth to power can destroy a writer as surely as mediocrity and compromise. *A Walk on the Wild Side*, the last of Algren's novels to be published in his lifetime, is in consequence a most moving achievement. It was an act of courage by a man no longer sure of his country, no longer certain of either his own worth or his relevance, convinced only that he had lost the woman who was the great love of his life.

A Walk on the Wild Side is in some ways a desperate attempt by a writer to reassure himself that he can still write, a writer like F. Scott Fitzgerald described himself as being in *The*

Crack-Up—a work at first something of a touch-stone for Nelson Algren and later a chronicle of a disintegration foretold—who feels that he has become less through his writing and, worse, that he has nothing left to write.

It is then a novel written against fate, by a writer who even at the height of his success in 1950 foresaw his own forlorn destiny as inextricably tied to his vocation as writer.

'Thinking of Melville,' he wrote, 'thinking of Poe, thinking of Mark Twain and Vachel Lindsay, thinking of Jack London and Tom Wolfe, one begins to feel there is almost no way of becoming a creative writer in America without being a loser.'

There are no second acts in American literature, Fitzgerald famously remarked, and so it was with Nelson Algren. *A Walk on the Wild Side* is the final scene in one of the more brilliant first acts in twentieth-century American writing.

Nelson Algren's irreparably American life tends to read like a novel by Nelson Algren. Compounding the impossible wrath of the gods was the impossible nature of the man born Nelson Algren Abraham in Detroit, 1909, the grandson of Nels Ahlgren, a Swedish adventurer possessed of the unrelenting strength of others' opinions. Nels Ahlgren converted to Judaism and became a self-appointed rabbi with the name of Isaac Ben Abraham, who emigrated first to the USA then, in 1870, to Jerusalem, where 'he chastised Jews for their lack of orthodoxy'.

The family made it back to the USA, where Nels Ahlgren deserted his family and became a mercenary missionary, preaching the faith of any group or sect willing to pay for his services. With characteristic perversity and some insight, Algren in his later life claimed to heavily identify with his grandfather.

'A man who won't demean himself for a dollar is a phoney to my way of thinking,' the late-middle-aged Algren wrote in a letter, an opinion consistent with the young Algren's conviction, taken from Whitman, that he belonged with the 'convicts and prostitutes', believing that in humiliation and degradation was to be found truth. The truth mattered to Algren, but it didn't help.

'Like all writers,' wrote his friend John Clellon Holmes, 'he believed that truth would carry everything before it, and like all writers he was baffled to discover that nothing could be further from the truth.'

Algren's family moved to Chicago when he was three, and he grew up in poverty on the South Side. Chicago was his first great passion, and the city was booming, aspiring to the title of First City of the Republic. By the mid-century it would all be over and Chicago in spectacular decline: 'What stopped it is a mystery,' wrote A. J. Liebling in the *New Yorker* in 1952, 'like what happened to Angkor Wat.'

'Loving Chicago,' said Algren, 'is like loving a woman with a broken nose.'

But at the beginning it was for Algren the city of Shoeless Joe Jackson and the White Sox scandal; of the One Big Union and Eugene Debs and impoverished neighbourhoods bounded by Eastern European nationality; of the greatest slaughterhouses in the continent and some of its most celebrated writers—Upton Sinclair, Theodore Dreiser, Sherwood Anderson and Carl Sandburg; of what he called the 'slander-coloured evening hour' and 'pavement-hued faces'. It was this city in its early twentieth-century struggles and urban romance that shaped Algren's vision of the USA.

Graduating as a journalist at the height of the depression in 1931, Algren headed south seeking work, and in 1932 landed in New Orleans, a city more Caribbean than North American, where girls 'were so hard pressed' they would let a man sleep with them if he bought them a pork sandwich. Later, in an abandoned Texas petrol station, Algren wrote his first short story that led to a book advance. He was subsequently imprisoned for stealing a typewriter.

He returned to Chicago and in 1935 his first novel was published, a gritty tale of a Texan drifter, which sold only 750 copies. Originally called *Native Son*, the title was changed by the publishers to the appalling *Somebody in Boots*, Algren's friend Richard Wright having the sense to later borrow the original title for what would become his most famous novel.

Algren's second novel, *Never Come Morning* (1942), was better received, and returning from the war in which he had served as stretcher bearer, Algren's star further rose with a collection of short stories, *The Neon Wilderness* (1947).

Algren's work was attracting attention for its unusual marriage of a sumptuous prose style and a dry humour, with subjects normally rendered in the dreariest of realistic and naturalistic tones: the lives of those at the bottom. Algren's world, in one of the many memorable phrases he brought into common usage (including 'walk on the wild side', 'monkey on the back' and 'I knew I'd never make it to twenty-one anyway') is 'a neon wilderness', and his novels can read like a natural history of American underlife.

Street corners, beerhalls, slum bedrooms, brothels and racetracks, police line-ups and prison cells become exotic habitats when described by Algren, and his stories play out to dramatic effect beneath arc lamps and twenty-watt bulbs (it's always too late in an Algren novel), in places 'filling with noises and rumours of noises', the rattle of freight cars, the hiss of downstairs laundry presses, the sound of far-off screams.

In 1949 came his first masterpiece, *The Man with the Golden Arm*. The story of a Chicago junkie trying to go straight was an immediate triumph. By 1950 Nelson Algren seemed destined for only ever greater things. *Never Come Morning* was on its way to being a million seller. In March 1950 *The Man with the Golden Arm* was awarded the first ever National Book Award, a hugely publicised event at that brief moment, now so long gone it is hard to imagine, when American novels seemed to be central to American culture and life. Algren was given the award under a blaze of lights by Eleanor Roosevelt.

'OK, kid,' Hemingway privately noted in his copy of *Man with the Golden Arm*, 'you beat Dosto-evsky', while publicly hailing Algren as the best American writer after Faulkner ('He said after Faulkner,' Algren commented later, 'I was very hurt.'). For a moment the man who celebrated loss had success as only America can bestow.

And then there was his love affair with one of the most famous European writers of the time: Simone de Beauvoir, who joked in a letter to Algren in 1949 while writing what became *The Second Sex* that she would call her new book *Never Come Woman*—'Is that not clear?'—a play on Algren's *Never Come Morning*.

De Beauvoir had met and fallen in love with Algren in Chicago in 1947. The affair continued off and on for several years. While de Beauvoir had a complex relationship with Jean-Paul Sartre, and Algren was a womaniser who had been unhappily married to Amanda Kontowicz for ten years, it does seem to have been on both writers' part a grand passion. In October 1947, following de Gaulle's election victory, Simone de Beauvoir wrote to the man she called 'her husband': 'I do not want to care for politics anymore. God let me live just some more years to love you and be loved by you.'

She goes on to write at letter end:

Dearest, beloved one, this letter seems so poor, reading it again. I should have put in it all my love and heart and body, all the autumn in Paris, the yellow trees, the peaceful sky, the feverish people. And just words. Dry words. But I hope you'll know how to read it; maybe you are smart enough to find in it all I wanted to put. Maybe you'll even find me. I'll wait for you, Nelson. I'll wait until you come to me.

But politics and history were undoing her 'beloved Chicago man' and their love affair. Gathering were the dark clouds of the Cold War. Against the determined conformism of the 1950s, the possibility of a nuclear winter, Red scares, growing blacklists and the emergence of McCarthyism, Algren's destiny irrevocably altered. The times were no longer his.

In a septic climate of rising fear, Algren used his celebrity to speak out—for the Hollywood Ten, for the Rosenbergs and against McCarthyism. In books such as *Chicago: the City on the Make* (1951) his writing continued to talk of the dark underbelly of the USA, in a voice ever richer and darker. In January 1951, Algren along with Arthur Miller and fifteen others placed a letter as an ad in the *New York Times* calling on people to speak up for freedom.

Half a century later the persecution of Algren that ensued is all the more terrifying for its insidious nature. As the FBI assembled a five-hundred-page dossier on Algren that could establish him guilty of nothing, as other writers went silent, *Life* magazine, a major force in American popular culture of the era, cancelled without explanation a major photo essay on Algren. In March 1953 his application for a passport to travel to France was denied by the State Department 'in light of his former connection to the Communist Party'. Algren, according to his friend Dave Peltz, now 'lived in terror . . . he would appear before the [House of Un-American Activities] Committee'.

In September 1953, Algren's publisher Doubleday refused to publish a short non-fiction book he
had written that in part attacked McCarthyism, an
extraordinary act given that at the time Algren was
one of the best known and most popular writers
in the USA. The book was not to be published
till nearly a quarter of a century later as *Nonconformity*—one of the strangest and most strangely
compelling meditations on writing by a twentieth-
century writer. In a clipped, laconic prose with
ironic jabs delivered in deftly told anecdotes,
Nonconformity maps out a duty, an aesthetic, a
politics that for Algren is also an inexorable destiny;
to swim against the current, to give everything, and
know it will destroy you as a writer.

It is an indictment of the American project
from a position inescapably American in its
humour, references and language. It is both the
final manifestation of the lost voices of a different
America—the America of Whitman and Twain
and Fitzgerald—and speaks to the future in its
attempt to remind its readers of an indigenous
tradition of American radicalism founded in the
experience of the lost and dispossessed.

Animating this book of fear and desire is his
love for Simone de Beauvoir, and some have seen
it as an attempt to prove to her that there was
a basis, political, artistic and intellectual, for a
radical writer in the USA.

At another level it is a writer weighing up the immense spiritual costs of writing: how one may write great works and in the end be less as a human being for the effort. This is the Algren who would shortly be writing *A Walk on the Wild Side*: lost, heartbroken, trying to hold on to the last thing he has, which is slipping through his very fingers as he types the next word: his belief writing might still matter in a country as lost as the USA, and that he still has something left to write for his country; a patriot who knows he is now viewed as a traitor.

At about the same time as *Nonconformity* was rejected, Algren began a novel called *Entrapment*, the story of which was based on the life of a heroin addict with whom he had an affair, but the emotional strength of which would seem to derive from his love for de Beauvoir. He could not get the novel moving.

His torment was only beginning. His marriage to Amanda seemed increasingly a matter to him of pity and not love, and, a compulsive gambler who seems invariably to have lost, he was losing large sums in poker games. His writing stalled and censored, his love affair with de Beauvoir transformed into an impossible anguish, despairing of his country, Algren wrote to de Beauvoir at the end of 1953 that he was depressed, and 'felt himself trapped by both money and marriage'. He felt he had become in every way, as he now signed his letters, 'the American prisoner'.

In 1955 came the experience of having *The Man with the Golden Arm* made into a film by Otto Preminger, an experience that left Algren feeling exploited and further depressed him. 'I went out there [Hollywood] for a thousand a week,' he was later to say, 'and I worked Monday, and I got fired Wednesday. The guy that hired me was out of town Tuesday.' He never went to see the movie, which he later described as 'my war with America as represented by Kim Novak'.

While living through all this Algren began *A Walk on the Wild Side*. Later in his life Algren would consider it his best novel, 'an American fantasy written to an American beat as true as Huckleberry Finn'. But at the beginning it was simply a way of making some easy money quickly, which he intended to use to escape his marriage and go to Paris.

In late 1953 he struck a deal with Doubleday to rewrite *Somebody in Boots* as a paperback, a hundred-dollar-a-week deal. Algren envisaged a 'good, cheap, corny' readers' book.

'No, it won't win any national book award,' Algren wrote in a letter. 'I'm aiming solely at the pocketbook traffic.'

But as he worked, the novel transformed: the original tragic tale of Cass McKay becomes the tragi-comedy of Dove Linkhorn, who drifts into New Orleans in 1931. He worked in some of his old short stories, and drew on some of his experiences from Depression-era New Orleans working scams.

Algren returned to New Orleans in the summer of 1954 but, finding it of little help, he went home to Chicago. There the novel now called *Finnerty's Ball* began to take shape, as Algren played 'The House of the Rising Sun' over and over, spending his spare time in the Chicago underworld or visiting Iris van Etten, a middle-class black woman on the South Side who was a madam, and in whose establishment Algren picked up stories for the novel's brothel scenes.

Whereas *The Man with the Golden Arm* was built, Algren said, sentence by sentence, the new novel, he said in an interview at the time, was 'plotted a great deal more than any other . . . I'm trying to write a reader's book, more than my own book . . . Mechanically and, I think, technically, it's done more carefully, and probably reads better than previous books.'

He finished the new novel, now called *A Walk on the Wild Side*, in November 1955, but Doubleday rejected the manuscript and demanded he repay his advance of $8000.

Having filed for divorce a few months earlier, he was unable to return to his home where

Amanda was living. Desperately reworking the book as he went, he later recalled how he 'had to write a book in flight—Montana, Saranac Lake, Baltimore, Havana, East St Louis'. He tried, he wrote, 'not to regret so much time taken from the book I'd begun', and with the money from the reprint rights he dreamed of getting 'back to my lonely life, and the book I'd begun before'.

Algren's own ambivalence about the new novel mirrored the growing ambivalence he felt about everything around and about him: his personal life, his prospects, his country.

'What country is there for a white man who isn't white?' Algren once asked. Maybe it was the Big Easy he created in *A Walk on the Wild Side*.

The novel begins with Dove Linkhorn, drifter, fleeing his Texan hometown after raping the Mexican woman who has deflowered him, evading a recruiting sergeant who wants to enlist him to fight Sandino in Nicaragua, and after some adventures coming 'at last to the town that always seems to be rocking', a fairytale place of speakeasies and flophouses full of 'old time sterno drinkers and bindlestiff nomads [who] made the flophouse forenoon murky with their hardtime breath'.

Dove Linkhorn is a good soldier, Schweik-like idiot with a dash of Tom Jones, an illiterate who goes to the segregated town's black toilets and drinks from the blacks only water fountains; who at one point gets attacked by a dog whose owner apologises: 'I never knowed Queenie to go after a white man before.' When seeking a job as scabbing seaman and asked if he belongs to a union, he declares, 'Mister, I'm a Christian boy and don't truckle to Yankee notions.'

In New Orleans, Dove Linkhorn finds work variously running scams, making condoms and as a stud in a peepshow, where he deflowers women pretending to be virgins, finally ending up in jail.

As if to mock the USA's yearnings, Algren attributes them in *A Walk on the Wild Side* to pimps, panders, whores and con men. In a society where people die of usefulness, Algren's inverted Big Easy is one where people 'died of uselessness one by one, yet lived on behind veritable prairie fires of wishes, hoping for something to happen that had never happened before: the siren screaming toward the crashing smash-up, the gasp of the man with the knife on his side, the suicide leap for no reason at all'. The true perversity of Algren's society is not sexual, but ethical: unlike the USA, where work is a virtue, here it is understood that 'nothing could lower human dignity faster than manual labour'.

Algren mocks the heroic, and his New Orleans is constantly upside down and comic. There is the white naval commander who is a self-confessed 'black mammie freak' and pays to be beaten by old black women. After thrashing him and taking a month's pay for her services, a black madam lowers herself onto a divan, sighs and then asks for the evening newspaper so she can see 'what the white folks are up to'.

The novel is at its most alive describing its ensemble casts of the brothels and jailhouse, for *A Walk on the Wild Side* is in the end not a novel about its hero, Dove Linkhorn, nor a naturalistic rendering, precisely drawn, of Depression-era New Orleans poverty. There is little sense of the physicality of New Orleans—its heat, its stench, its polyglot nature. For all Algren's belief in detail, his retelling of his own New Orleans experiences, this is no more a realistic world than that of Rabelais. But with it Algren created a uniquely American vision that questioned the essence of America, embodying a vision of truth that seems strikingly contemporary in its resonance. In consequence, the book is not what it sets out to be, and its structure is sometimes looser than its language.

What remains are such telling scenes as the one in which Dove Linkhorn visits a cave-like restaurant, where he watches a pyramid of snapping turtles blindly climbing on top of each other, only to then be beheaded by a black man naked to the waist who grabs the next topmost turtle for decapitation, a symbol of the USA's pointless, destructive yearnings.

'When we get more houses than we can live in, more cars than we can ride in, more food than we can eat ourselves, the only way of getting richer is by cutting off those who don't have enough,' writes Algren, describing his true subject best.

Dove Linkhorn, Kitty Twist, Legless Schmidt, Oliver Finnerty, Reba, Hallie and a large collection of those Algren calls 'the broken men and breaking ones; wingies, dingies, zanies and lopsided kukes; cokies and queers and threadbare whores' are all in search of the USA, only for the reader to discover in the end they are the USA.

A Walk on the Wild Side was finally published by Farrar, Straus and Cudahy in May 1956. The hit of Broadway at the time was a new Cinderella story called *My Fair Lady*. The times could hardly have been less propitious.

The reviews of *A Walk on the Wild Side* have become legendary in their savagery; at times they seem as politically charged in their circumlocutions as any Soviet review of the era of writers deemed unacceptable by the state. There were some who defended the novel, but they were drowned out by the novel's detractors.

Time Magazine declared that Algren's 'sympathy for the depraved and degraded has not carried him to the edge of nonsense . . . Algren has dressed his sense of compassion in the rags of vulgarity'. In the *New Yorker* Norman Podhoretz attacked what he called Algren's 'boozy sentimentality' and claimed that Algren was saying 'we live in a society whose bums and tramps are better men than the preachers and the politicians and the otherwise respectable'.

Leslie Fiedler similarly claimed that there was no room in Algren's world for 'workers or teachers or clerks' and went on to describe Algren as 'isolated from the life of his time. He was made, unfortunately, once and for all in the early 1930s in the literary cult of "experience" of those times. He has not thought a new thought or felt a new feeling since . . . as our literature has moved on and left him almost a museum piece—the Last of the Proletarian Writers.'

The political crime was unmistakeable, as the verdict and punishment were inescapable. Book sales fell away. Though he continued to write and publish, Nelson Algren was finished. His novels went out of print, he was neglected, his reputation diminished to the extent that for a time he was largely forgotten. It is hard to think of a major American writer of similar stature who has had so little impact on subsequent American writing.

Algren sensed the change—how could he not?—and the way in which critics were increasingly not on the side of the artist, but the status quo. In 1960 he wrote of the new owners of literature, arriving 'directly from their respective campuses armed with blueprints to which the novel and the short story would have to conform . . . [forming] a loose federation, between the literary quarterlies, publishers' offices and book review columns, presenting a view of American letters untouched by American life'. The New Criticism—with its emphasis on the search for imagery, symbols and metaphors, and its contempt for history and politics in shaping art—was for Algren a tragic misunderstanding of the role of literature; for 'it left unheeded the truth that the proper study of mankind is man'.

In some way the criticisms of 1956 have mutated but remain: the charge that Algren was an overwrought word-drunk boozed up on an outdated sentimentality stuck. That he was a relic from the thirties; that the world had changed and Algren had not.

It is too simple to say that Algren was punished for his politics. His politics, left-leaning though they were, were not his real crime. Algren understood far better than those who blackballed him the nature of his offence.

His aesthetics were not what the new empire wanted: what was emerging, what was wanted was a new classicism: a pared-back modernist prose. Nor was his subject—the dispossessed—any longer of interest or concern.

'I think Faulkner is too tragic about life,' Simone de Beauvoir wrote to Nelson Algren. 'Life is tragic, and it is not. In your books one can feel very well this strange two-sided truth.' But in a nation whose culture seemed ever more hostile to irony, tragi-comic art had less and less place.

Not the least of Nelson Algren's charms to those of us not American is the way he is at once both entirely of the USA in all its extraordinary vibrancy, and yet able to tally and report accurately and honestly the immense human cost of that vibrancy: a USA not just a dream of exploding possibility, but also a nightmare of receding hopes.

'The pimps,' he wrote of 1930s New Orleans in *A Walk on the Wild Side*, 'didn't seem to catch on that the country was progressing downward to new rates of normality.'

And Algren achieved all this in a lush language at once immediate and vernacular, but steeped in the tradition of his culture's greatest writers: the poetry of his sentences harked back to Whitman; his wry humour and vernacular power to Twain; his novelistic largeness to Melville; his pained humanity to Fitzgerald.

But everything in Algren is transformed into a particularly American agony, comic and tragic, and he created an idea of a spiritually compromised USA so potent that for some decades no one wished to know of it.

Frequently categorised, with the passage of years no category seems sufficient to label the rich, fecund world of Algren's greatest works. He was a naturalist who wrote unnaturalistic prose; an absurdist whose work reeked of reality; a realist whose best effects are often comic, a determined stylist who in the end believed passion mattered more than style, a passionate writer who fully understood that the measure of great writing was in its capacity to escape the writer's intentions, politics and passions.

Those who ascribed to him a program, an ideology, failed to understand Algren's humility in the face of the power of art to tell truths often unknown to the artist and even unpalatable to them. He believed good writing came out of compulsions unknown to the writer.

'A writer who knows what he is doing,' he once said, 'isn't doing very much.'

Algren's characters fail even at failure: they manage to mismanage crime, vice, sin; nothing is so worthless that it cannot be lost; and Algren's mean streets are revealed by the passing of time to be both as real and as allegorical as Kafka's court-rooms and castles. It is a hell, and it is the ultimate test of our humanity.

It would be too simple to see Algren as a victim of the Cold War. His literature threw down a question to the fundamental nature of the USA.

'So accustomed have we become to the testimony of the photo-weeklies, backed by witnesses from radio and TV,' Algren wrote, 'establishing us permanently as the happiest, healthiest, sanest, wealthiest, most inventive, tolerant and fun-loving folk yet to grace the earth of man, that we tend to forget that these are bought-and-paid-for witnesses and all their testimony perjured.'

The American dream, the American century, the American way, the American empire: Algren didn't buy any of it. The USA, Algren declared in an interview in 1963, was 'an imperialist son-of-a-bitch', and Algren did not conceive the role of the writer to sing of its triumphs.

'The hard necessity of bringing the judge on the bench down into the dock,' Algren wrote, 'has been the peculiar responsibility of the writer in all ages of man.'

Like Chekhov, Algren believed a writer's role was to side with the guilty.

'American literature is the woman in the courtroom who, finding herself undefended on a charge, asked, "Isn't anyone on my side?" . . . More recently I think American literature is also the fifteen-year-old who, after he had stabbed somebody, said, "Put me in the electric chair—my mother can watch me burn."'

And so Algren wrote with courage and love against the grain of the American empire he clearly recognised coming into being around him, as doomed as a bard of slaves would have been in first-century Rome.

'The American middle class's faith in personal comfort as an end in itself is in essence a denial of life,' Algren wrote in *Nonconformity*. 'And it has been imposed upon American writers and play-wrights strongly enough to cut them off from their deeper sources.'

According to his friend Kurt Vonnegut, 'No matter how famous he became, he remained a poor man living among the poor, and usually alone.' But there was about this something that went beyond identification or Algren's belief in people. For Algren it seems that it also enabled a form of spiritual transcendence that he found necessary in order to write.

'Innocence is not just the lack of something,' Algren once said. 'Innocence is an achieved thing. You can't be unworldly without first being worldly . . . to be an innocent in the best sense is to have that kind of unworldliness that comes out of worldliness, to be able to see how people waste their whole lives just to have security.'

The American Dream was one of materialism. Its hope was that even if you had lost everything yesterday you might regain your fortune today. Algren's dream is one of humanity; of how you might live a fully human life when you have lost everything and nothing can be regained: through humour, through small victories, through love of others.

In the wake of the critical and commercial failure of *A Walk on the Wild Side*, Algren's life took an increasingly tragic turn.

The same month as it appeared, a literary sensation from Europe received its first US publication. *The Mandarins*, Simone de Beauvoir's new novel dedicated to Algren, in part described a passionate affair between its heroine and an American writer called Lewis Brogan, clearly modelled on Algren. What to de Beauvoir was an affirmation of their love, was to Algren, who had quarried the lives of others, a personal betrayal, and Algren now attacked de Beauvoir in the press. Yet privately he still hoped to escape to Paris and de Beauvoir.

On 26 June 1956 this dream was cruelly ended when his passport was once more denied. On 1 July 1956 he rang de Beauvoir and apologised, though he was to attack her again publicly. On 12 July 1956 she wrote to Algren how 'in *The Mandarins*, the love story is very different from the true truth; I just tried to convey something of it. Nobody understands that when the man and woman love each other for ever, they are still in love and maybe this love will never die.'

Now a deeply depressed man, Algren returned to what had been his own home in Gary and asked

Amanda Kontowicz to take him in. There he spent most of his days sitting in his room, unable to work, often weeping. In August, he suffered a breakdown that led him to being hospitalised.

'Amanda called me,' Dave Peltz recalled in a radio interview many years later, 'and she said, he's ready, he wants, he's going to allow himself to be put into hospital care, and I came over to the house . . . he was half-dressed, he wouldn't put on a shirt, and then he put on his shirt, then he wouldn't put on his jacket, then he put on the jacket, he wouldn't put his shoes on, then he put his shoes on and finally, after an hour, I said I have to go. He got dressed and he sat in the car.

'We drove all the way north to this psychiatric hospital, got out, went into the lobby and he was supposed to sign in, he wouldn't sign in . . . He would make an "S". He took an "N", he made an "S", he would make an "A" over here, and then come back and put an "E" in between the "N" and the "L", and after an interminable two hours he filled in his name, and the minute he did that, it was like in a B movie.

'Two guys in white coats came out and they just literally picked him up and hauled him right through a big solid core door, and, as they're doing that, he's hollering "Dave! Dave!" And they took him through the hallway and I could hear him hollering "Dave!" And I'll tell you it's still in my ears, that scream, that "Dave!".'

At the end of 1956 Simone de Beauvoir received a letter from her beloved Chicago man saying a light had gone out in him.

He had abandoned *Entrapment*—the novel he had stolen time from to finish *A Walk on the Wild Side*. Of its unfinished manuscript a later editor of Algren's, William Targ, said, 'In it he seemed to reach the deep-down essence of the blackest lower depths: drugs, pimping, prostitution, at their most grim level . . . It would have been an extraordinary achievement . . . it could have been his major opus.'

According to Sylvie Le Bon de Beauvoir, Simone's daughter, who has possession of these Algren letters, Algren confessed he had 'hit rock bottom, having lost himself in draining battles against his marriage, his publishers, his agents, his lawyers and his poverty. He felt he had lost his driving force, the spark fuelling his writing and his entire being. He realised he was losing Simone de Beauvoir forever, and in this dire mood was not afraid to admit that he missed her terribly. The best days of his life were spent with her. Why had he let her drift so far away?'

On 31 December 1956 he took a shortcut across a frozen lagoon, the ice broke, and Algren would have died in its freezing waters, had he not been rescued by workmen. Close friends speculated that Algren had tried to kill himself.

Of the remaining twenty-five years of Algren's life there is little to tell. Though he wrote more books, including one posthumously published novel, the great creative period of his life was over. Like the police captain Record Head Bednar in *The Man with the Golden Arm*, obsessed with the sense he should write his own name on the list of the guilty, Nelson Algren had ended up inscribing his own name on the guilty list, the black list, then the reviled and finally the lost and forgotten list. He took to calling himself a journalist, rather than a novelist.

'The past is a bucket of ashes,' he told friends.

Algren laughed in the face of the gods, made merry, but his fate is no less tragic for his own particular enduring courage.

In later years Nelson Algren gave the impression that there was nothing he wanted more out of life than to see a fight, or go to the track, or play poker.

'This was pose, of course,' Kurt Vonnegut has written, 'and perceived as such by one and all.'

But it was pose with a price, and pose with a point. The poverty, the gambling, the losing continued; the novel writing did not; he posed, until, one suspects, the pose became too fixed to escape.

'For years he was exhausted,' Dave Peltz has said, 'trying to get over what he had done with

his life, what he had done with this great opportunity that he had, and many people described
him as America's foremost writer . . . He felt he
blew it, something happened in his life [and]
that he blew it . . . towards the end when he was
not writing all he thought about was fame and
fortune, like someone who went to the crap table
and lost it all. I think gambling was the metaphor
for his life, for pissing away his life . . . he stayed
disciplined in the early days before he achieved
success and somehow after success was when he
lost hold, and I can't account for it. Unless . . .
he needed to be consistent with being a loser,
needed to be consistent with having a pocket full
of money and going to a crap table and losing it.'

Nelson Algren died in 1981, Simone de Beauvoir
in 1986. She was buried with the ring Algren had
given her.

Algren's epitaph for Fitzgerald could apply
equally to himself:

Unsaving of spirit and heart and brain, he
served the lives of which he wrote rather than
allowing himself to be served by them.

And so he died like a scapegoat, died like a
victim, his work unfinished, his hopes in ruin.

The USA was at the time of Algren's childhood a symbol of an ideal that could still seem

revolutionary and democratic. For Whitman, a seminal influence on Algren, American democracy was a new event; for Algren it is one more lost cause in a life devoted to lost causes, the greatest of which was writing, the act of which demanded you spend of your soul until there is nothing left but the prospect of death.

The fiftieth anniversary of the publication of *A Walk on the Wild Side* takes on an odd resonance given the recent tragic events in what was the Big Easy, not only because the town is the setting for the novel, but because Algren's principal concern—the USA's contempt for so many of its own people—is, perhaps for the first time since the 1930s, threatening to become a major political issue. In rebuilding the levies of New Orleans, Americans could do worse than reread *A Walk on the Wild Side*.

And not only they.

'Vast populations, towering cities, erroneous and clamorous publicity, have conspired to make unknown great men one of America's traditions,' Borges wrote. 'Edgar Allan Poe was one of these; so was Melville.' And so too Nelson Algren.

Introduction, Nelson Algren,
A Walk on the Wild Side (2006)

Soviet Man

In 1962, the writer Vasily Grossman met with Mikhail Suslov, chief ideologue of the USSR's Politburo. The KGB had confiscated all known manuscripts of Grossman's epic novel of World War II, *Life and Fate*.

Once one of the most celebrated Russian war journalists, once an acclaimed novelist, the now disgraced Grossman was dying of stomach cancer. He had come to beg Suslov that the book be published.

Suslov told Grossman that his novel was more damaging to the USSR than Pasternak's *Dr Zhivago*. It could not be published, said Suslov, for two hundred years.

Unknown to either Grossman or the KGB, one of Grossman's friends had made a secret copy.

Nearly twenty years after Grossman's death, it was smuggled out of the USSR. Though it made little impact on publication in Switzerland in 1980, it has in the decades since come to be hailed as a twentieth-century *War and Peace*, and with this changing fortune, Grossman has secured a reputation as a latter-day Tolstoy.

All praise is a form of misunderstanding, and Grossman is a writer more difficult than most to divine. Unlike the great Soviet writers who were products of pre-Revolutionary Russia—Babel, Bulgakov, Mandelstam, Pasternak, Akhmatova— Grossman was a product of the new order, an insider, a Soviet man.

Everything he had, he wrote in a letter to the NKVD chief Yeshov begging for the release— really, the life—of his arrested wife, 'I owe to the Soviet government.'

Why this man—a conformist who made his accommodations with the Soviet tyranny, turned his back, averted his eye, held his tongue, signed accusing letters—came to a point where he said No to his masters is perhaps unknowable.

Certainly his experience of the war, his witnessing of the Holocaust, the death of his mother at the hands of the Einsatzgruppen, Stalin's post-war anti-Semitic campaign, his discovery of love in middle age—a large life, in short, that cannot be detailed here—led Grossman to finally conclude that Fascism was simply a mirror response to the 'cosmic violence' of Soviet Communism. But why this then liberated him into writing two masterpieces of the twentieth century remains mysterious.

A few months after his meeting with Suslov, at the height of the Cuban missile crisis on 26 October 1962, the Central Committee heard that Grossman was at work on a new 'anti-Soviet' novel. The informer is suspected to be his stepson, who lived with Grossman.

As the world teetered on the abyss, Grossman's novel was discussed at the highest levels of Soviet leadership. Is it possible to imagine any book bequeathed such strange honour, such fear, today?

That novel was at the time of his death in 1964 unfinished. It was perhaps unfinishable. Yet in the abyss between ambition and failure often lies greatness. So it is with *Everything Flows*, in its way as remarkable an achievement as *Life and Fate*.

Yet when first published in English in 1972 as *Forever Flowing*, translated by Thomas Whitney, the translator of *The Gulag Archipelago*, the novel failed to garner anything like the attention that Solzhenitsyn had in the West. Grossman's idea of history was heretical to almost all. He didn't compare or rank the horrors of the Gulag and collectivisation or the Holocaust. Rather, and most chillingly, he connected them.

His anti-politics, of a type that anticipated the great revolts of the 1980s, rendered his work undivineable for many. The book offered neither succour to the left, in breaking the ultimate taboo of revering Lenin and Leninism, nor to the right, by offering a damning critique of pre-revolutionary Russia.

His humanism, placing kindness and goodness, truth and freedom, at the centre of life, as both the meaning and fullest expression of life, seemed weak, even quaint in the face of the cocaine rush of turbo-capitalism that took all before it in the final decades of the twentieth century with its material wonders and ideological triumph.

This new translation of Grossman's last novel by Robert Chandler is more poetic, more lyrical than Whitney's original translation. It is better, but not fundamentally different.

What has changed, perhaps, is us.

Suddenly, this story seems not about another world many years ago, but speaks to our world now and tomorrow.

The novel is ostensibly simple and could hardly be simpler. A man returns to society in 1957, after thirty years as a zek in the Gulag. He visits a friend, meets the man who betrayed him, finds a menial job as a metal worker, boards in a house and falls in love with his landlady, a war widow, who tells him her story of the Ukrainian famine consequent on Stalin's collectivisation policy, before she dies of lung cancer.

So far, one might think, so very Russian.

Within it, though, is a book constantly breaking boundaries, flooding over, travelling far from the strange anti-socialist realist, social realist *Life and Fate*; pointing to the great philosophical novels of Kundera, constantly keeping faith with the idea of story as the vehicle of truth.

There is an almost unbearably sad chapter—unrelated to anything else in the book, yet wholly integral to the novel—of a woman zek who dies after hearing dance music coming from a gaoler's cottage and who realises that her husband has been shot, that she will never see her daughter again, and that there is no hope.

Then there is the story of the cannibal mother who eats her two children, is tried and shot. 'We are all cannibals,' observes Grossman. About a loving couple, two Ukrainian collective farm workers and their child who starve to death and whose 'skeletons spent the winter together . . . smiling whitely, not separated even by death'.

And perhaps most extraordinary, a sympathetic portrait of the monstrous Jewish commissar Lev Mekler, from the shtetl of Fastov, the man who becomes the Commissar of Justice for the entire Ukraine, a romantic, even saintly figure in his torn leather jacket and Budyonny helmet with a red star 'that had faded as if from loss of blood', who brings suffering and death everywhere.

Mekler is faithful to the Revolution even after the Revolution 'had put him in a cell in the Lubyanka and knocked out eight of his teeth'. 'His faith did not waver when he lay on the floor and saw the polished toe of a box-calf boot beside his blood-filled mouth.'

Grossman compares Mekler's fate to that of a loyal dog whose owner hates it for its love.

'This is what is so terrifying: that there is so much good in them, so much good in their human essence,' writes Grossman. 'Whom then should we judge? Human nature?'

The book contains multitudes, and not only of people. Its moods range from the near mystical, in its depiction of women, particularly mothers; to hard political, in its study of Lenin; to epic and elegiac. Grossman somehow penetrates to the essence of the USSR in a way few ever did—alive to the psychology and the humanity of its revolutionaries, cannibals, zeks, commissars and secret policemen. Its pitiless descriptions of the horrors of the Ukraine famine make one shudder today; I suspect they will have the same effect in centuries to come.

'All the living are guilty,' he writes, a judgement he did not exclude himself from. He had signed the letters, he had refused to help, and he bore especial guilt about his mother, whom he felt he should have saved from the Holocaust.

The dying Grossman is a novelist now going for broke. Like the dying Bulgakov writing *The Master and Margarita*, he was liberated from fame, success, even the possibility of publication, to finally be able to write what he meant.

Near its end, *Everything Flows* breaks its banks again and again, chapters grow shorter, more concentrated, reducing history, thought, human nature, to a dazzling and dizzying poetry.

Grossman makes a chilling historical argument replete with the ultimate Soviet blasphemy, the essence of which is still shocking to come to terms with. That it was written half a century ago makes it even more extraordinary.

Grossman argues that the great nineteenth-century Russian prophets, from Gogol to Dostoevsky, those prophets of the unique Russian soul, believed that this soul, once fully realised, would lead the world to spiritual evolution.

The fatal flaw, according to Grossman, was that 'all failed to see that this soul had been enslaved for a thousand years'.

For Grossman, Russian history was a chronicle of slavery. He traces the growing enslavement of the Russian people through the Middle Ages, and argues that the great progressive achievements of Peter the Great and Catherine the Great were linked to a corresponding increase in the growth of what he calls 'non-freedom'.

In Russia, Grossman sees progress and slavery as inextricably linked, while in the West it is progress and the growth of freedom.

And here is the heart of Grossman's terrifying vision: the true consequences of Lenin's revolution were to take this uniquely Russian slavery to the world. This for Grossman is the Russian spectacle that enchants the world: 'of modernisation through non-freedom'.

For Grossman, Stalin is but a consequence, and an inevitable one at that, of Lenin. And not just Stalin, but Fascism. Writing this in the early 1960s in Russia was more than merely blasphemous. It was an historical insight of extraordinary perception.

'Did Russia's prophets ever imagine,' Grossman wrote in the final months of his life, 'that their prophecies about the coming universal triumph of the Russian soul would find their grating fulfilment in the unity of the barbed wire stretched around Auschwitz and the labour camps of Siberia?'

Grossman's hero, Ivan Grigoryevich, senses the spirit of the Gulag all around him. 'Barbed wire, it seemed, was no longer necessary; life outside the barbed wire had become in its essence no different from that of the barracks.'

How terrifying this insight is: an idea has escaped the Gulag and might take the world.

The great irony, according to Grossman, was that Lenin, through his violence and terror, not just destroyed any possibility of liberation from what he terms 'the satanic force of Russia's serf past', but.hugely advanced its domain. 'Through the will, passion and genius of Lenin, Russia's thousand-year law of development became a worldwide law.'

And who looking at China can read this without trembling? Who can contemplate the USA's present stumblings and the rise of the Tea Party movement without wondering?

'A Putin–Palin ticket,' suggested Gary Shteyngart—another Russian–Jewish writer whose contemporary satires focus on turbo-capitalism's closeness to old-style totalitarianism—'can really cement the liberties Russia has achieved over the last two hundred years.'

Yet as he journeys through hell, somehow Grossman divines meaning in all this, and is finally hopeful. He concludes that freedom can never be destroyed. For Grossman this is 'a sacred law of life: human freedom stands above everything. There is no end in this world for the sake of which it is permissible to sacrifice human freedom.'

When he died, two letters were found in Grossman's shirt pocket. One was the last letter his mother sent him from north Ukraine before the invading Germans murdered her, along with 30,000 other Jews of Berdichev in 1941. The other letter is his reply to his mother's letter, written in 1951. In a sense he never stopped writing that letter.

Chekhov, the grandson of a serf, wrote what could well serve as Grossman's epitaph:

> Write about this man who, drop by drop, squeezes the slave's blood out of himself until he wakes one day to find the blood of a real human being—not a slave's—coursing through his veins.

Grossman, one senses, died a free man.

The Age
18 September 2010

And What Do You Do, Mr Gable?

NEAR THE END of making the movie of *One Hand Clapping*, I one night stayed back in the cutting room drinking with my editor, John Scott, whose luminous career span's the history of modern Australian film. I listened to his wondrous tales of film-making madness: of directors whose productions had run out of money and who burnt their out-takes both to keep warm and so that they could not be made to put them back in their final cut; of actors who got drunk and surly in order to provoke fights they then lost in order to play in a suitably physically decrepit manner a death scene the following day; of producers imprisoned for stealing art works to finance their next film.

He told me of how for every tired Hollywood joke about the tycoon who comes to Beverly Hills and sends his chauffeur in to the hotel to bring back the most expensive whore he can find, only for the chauffeur then to return with a writer, there is an apocryphal tale of encounters such as that between Clark Gable and William Faulkner, traditionally scripted as follows:

CLARK GABLE:
And what do you do, Mr Faulkner?
WILLIAM FAULKNER:
I write. And what do you do,
Mr Gable?

When I went home that evening, I had on my bedside table Joseph Roth's 1924 novel *Hotel Savoy*, set in a hotel on the border between Europe and Russia after World War I. The book fell open to the page in which the narrator, a survivor of Siberian POW camps, watched endless masses of refugees and soldiers flooding in from the revolution- and war-torn east, while from the West came 'loud people who shouted and lied at the top of their voices, so as to deafen their conscience. They were cheats and braggarts and all of them came from the film industry and had a lot to tell about the world, but they saw the world through their goggle eyes, held it to be a commercial failure on

the part of God, and intended to compete with him
and to go into business on an equally large scale.'

Near a century has passed and Roth's goggle-
eyed cheats and braggarts may not yet have
overtaken God, but they have become, in their
own words, king of the world, while the refugees
continue to flood in from the east, and, like a
hopelessly feuding old couple, writers and film-
makers continue to denigrate each other, and
continue to need each other.

For my own part, I have come to a somewhat
different position than is conventional. For one,
I don't believe in the myth of the devouring maw
of movies. For another, I learnt a great deal from
my time in the industry, about people as well as
art, about how to tell stories, about rhythm, about
narration—lessons I am still absorbing. And it has
long seemed to me a gross slander to suggest, when
film fails to deliver on the promise of the written
word—be it a novel or a play or a screenplay—that
it is writers who have been uniquely betrayed in
the film-making process.

Because in the film industry everyone is
betrayed, everyone is exploited, and the writer
differs only in his ludicrous individual vanity, in
thinking that his pitiful situation is unique to him,
rather than common to all. I say this with the
sorry authority of one who is a writer by trade, but
a director by misadventure.

I had never directed a centimetre of celluloid in my life, had no background in film-making whatsoever, but I was guilty of writing one script, which had a long and curious history that culminated in me being asked if I wished to direct it.

Carlos Fuentes once remarked, 'We cannot act without the horizon of failure constantly in view.' Bearing this in mind and, in any case, having no other prospects of employment at the time, I agreed. Such vainglorious ignorance and its entirely predictable consequences are what the ancients coined the word hubris to explain, and invented classical comedy and tragedy to explore.

A director, Orson Welles said, is someone who presides over disasters. Welles' maxim captures perfectly the lunacy of the job, the King Canute-like nature of the role—to be granted seeming absolute power over events that can never be controlled, which, tide-like, wash up the shore over the feet, regardless of our desires, heedless of our demands. He neglected to add that the writer is the one who initiates the disaster, but that they should not be held responsible for its consequences.

As director I was to learn that film-making runs on terror, rewards mediocrity, and views everybody as expendable. Film-making is the closest thing to a totalitarian society we have left outside of North

Korea, and in it the director is expected to play the part of Kim Jong-Il. But it is only a part, and the director's job is closer to that of the actor than the artist, more the Wizard of Oz inflating his image than Stalin exercising his omnipotence—for power, as he is constantly reminded, does not reside with him but with his masters.

If the director is unwilling to play his role as dictator, he is seen as unfit for the job. If he is humble and good-natured, his humility and good nature will be understood only as weakness, and weakness will inevitably be punished. If he speaks honestly in a world in which the currency is lies, he destabilises not the tyranny, but only his own legitimacy as director. His position is hopeless, his task forlorn, his world a velvet prison.

He must suffer the politics of film—in which he is but a lackey—and the inevitable artistic costs of those politics with what the Russian writer Isaac Babel termed, in a speech in Moscow in 1934, as the authority of silence. The great Russian director Eisenstein wished to make films in the spirit in which Babel wrote: but in the end Babel's only possible answer to the horror of Stalinism was to write nothing, his creative death anticipating his physical death in the Gulag five short years later.

Film is troubled by these and by so many other things. It is troubled by needing too much money, and never having enough. It is troubled by wanting to be art and needing to be popular. It is troubled by needing too many people and it is troubled by the people it gets: a procession of the halt and the lame staggering back from a World War I killing field would have fewer physical and emotional traumas than the average film crew.

And film is troubled by the destructive delusion, shared by so many film-makers and writers, that film can and should aspire to the same condition as the written word. Film's desire for respectability remains strong after a century, and in consequence so does its ambition to put itself on a pedestal along with the older forms of storytelling, notably novels. Given that film's possibilities and delights are not those of the word, such a snobbery is both artistically destructive and historically ironic.

Three centuries ago it was novels that were dismissed as vulgar, common entertainments with neither artistic merit nor potential. Then justification for novels was sought through inappropriate comparisons and imitations of lyric poetry, as films today too often seek to justify their worth through an inappropriate deference to novels.

In film, fidelity to the written word is not necessarily desirable, even if it were realisable— which it is not. Such tensions between the word and the finished film are nothing new. In the screenplay for the original version of *King Kong* we find such descriptions as the following of Skull Island at dawn:

> The rose light of the silent domes flushes that heaven about them until the whole sky, one scarlet canopy, is interwoven with a roof of waving flame.

The first *King Kong* was shot in black and white.

Even great directors sometimes succumb to what may be termed the literary fallacy. In the screenplay for *Three Colours: Blue*, we read the following direction by the writer–director Krzysztof Kieślowski, for the character Julie to enter a doorway that 'is hideous and stinks'.

I still watch *Blue* hoping my nostrils might pick up that scent of Kieślowski's doorway.

It is a commonplace that screenplays are never the finished work: they are the invitation to others to build a finished work—the film—on a foundation of words. To direct is to learn something more—that a script is like a song tune that can be sung in many different ways. It is to discover that there is an infinite array of films, magnificent, average, mediocre and bad, that could be made from a single script. A writer tends to think there is only one version—the one he saw as he was writing.

In any case, whatever the intentions of the director and his colleagues, film remains above all else the art of the possible. It has been put to me that film is a cyclone you summon into existence, and in the eye of which you are compelled to live and work, hoping that it doesn't destroy both you and your movie before its energy is spent. Like all evocative metaphors this says in too many words what can be said simply in fewer: that film changes because of life.

Because of sickness. Love. Hate. Jealousy. Generosity. Technical fiascos. Bad weather. Genius. Mediocrity. Because a great scene on paper becomes a terrible scene on film when an actor has been up all night drinking and believes himself to be in the scene from the day before and that he is shortly to be murdered. Or the crew are in mutinous ferment because the first is out of her mind on cocaine because her boyfriend believes she is sleeping with the actor who is receiving death threats on his mobile phone. When the gaffer is being interviewed by police to assist with their enquiries regarding all or any of the above.

Occasionally, things do change for the better. For example, my brief for my film's composer, Cezary Skubiszewski, was limited and limiting. His wondrous music was neither, and when coupled with images, created effects and moods I had not been able to achieve with words. I found actors who would have wept tears of blood for a director if they knew how, who blew the breath of life into the dust of the dialogue and instructions that were my poor script.

Such miracles—the word seems not unjustified—of working together with gifted people were for me the great pleasure of film-making, and one of the great creative joys of my life. As a writer one more or less knows what one is capable of creating. The mystery of film is that you can never predict how much worse or how much better the final product will be from your original conception, because you are working with others.

And so film is not made in a state of inspiration when the muse and artist and environment come together in glorious creative ferment. Film is what you achieve with a small army of skilled anarchists embroiled in constant civil war, without enough money, running out of time, in a state of exhaustion, when you daily face the possibility you may be sacked.

There is, of course, the lamentable nonsense that because movies are a collaborative form, they are somehow superior as art to older individual forms such as the novel, being—supposedly—truer to the collective Zeitgeist. We may question this view if for a moment we ponder a short list of some of the truly great and successful collaborations of the last one hundred or so years: the genocide of the Armenians, the collectivisation of the kulaks, the Final Solution, Year Zero, Operation Desert Storm and *Star Wars: The Phantom Menace*. I offer no moral gloss on *The Phantom Menace*, nor yet an aesthetic one on the other listings. I would merely observe that collaboration is in itself neither a moral nor an aesthetic virtue, and should never, in any case, be taken as a guarantee that the final collectively realised product—the film—will be better than its individually conceived inspiration—the novel or screenplay.

There is the recurrent MacGuffin, as Hitchcock termed red herrings, that audiences relate to film as they do to novels. But where a novel written with no money can hold a reader transfixed for a dozen hours—in the bath, in bed, over breakfast, in a rattling, overcrowded tram—a film cannot. It needs the most elaborate technology available and even then has to lock people up in a state of sensory deprivation to keep them vaguely amused for a hundred minutes.

Could this have something to do with the way a novel demands that a reader collaborate in its creation, where a film does not? With the way a novel needs a reader to invent it as much as the writer; whereas a film dictates to an audience what the characters look like, sound like, and so on? Is a novel a cosmos we invent, and a film a cul-de-sac we only visit?

We are deluded by the budgets, the publicity, that vast screen, those extraordinary effects, to believe that the world is being shown us in the cinema. But in truth, a film is very limited in the story it can tell. A film structurally is a short story with, hopefully, some poetic overlays. It must cleave closely to its plot, and to a very small number of characters.

A novel, however, is a universe you must invent and people, and it is a much larger, richer and more diverse creation. I don't mean that novels are superior as a form, but that films, like sonnets, have definite constraints that one must understand and respect, and that, like sonnets, within those constraints anything is possible.

When writers write books, they write them without interference. No one in publishing threatens a writer that they may be taken off their book unless they write the next chapter like Wilbur Smith, because Wilbur's selling this week. No one says that they love the writing but the problem with this book is the writer. But in films, such heavy-handed behaviour—and far worse besides—is routine. And all because a book may be cheap, but a film is not.

In film, money is everything, and everyone ends up in its thrall. In comparison to any other art form, the money the film industry spends just on promoting and marketing itself is enormous, and makes me sometimes wonder whether film, rather than being the great art form, is instead the great hype, the great con job of our age. And yet it is undeniable that in spite of all arrayed against them, film-makers still sometimes manage to make great movies, but it is art made in a tyranny, and the name of the tyrant is money.

Novels, on the other hand, remain one of the last places where a single voice can speak the truth, untrammelled by the dictates of power and money, and still be heard across countries and over time. And this is because while books need a small amount of money to be published, they need no money to be written, whereas even a cheap film needs a great deal—several millions of dollars—to be made. In an ever more unfree age, when avenues for the expression of truth are daily closing off all around, this seems a not unimportant distinction, and one that will ensure books have a greater, rather than lesser, role and significance in the new world being born around us.

Still, when asked why he was writing soap operas following his Nobel Prize, Gabriel García Márquez replied, 'The medium is an invitation.' Very occasionally, I chance upon a movie that reminds me that in a situation of adversity, a few film-makers still attempt to craft an answer to their invitation with some worth and honour.

That they sometimes fail doesn't worry me.

'A man's reach should exceed his grasp, or what's a heaven for,' as the poet Browning once wrote. Browning is forgotten today, except when wielded as a pistol in yet one more Tarantino-esque standoff. No one reads poetry, and the one art that still has the capacity to reach millions too often works in the opposite direction. Though film's talk is incessantly and insidiously of the stars, its trajectory, the desired home of so many who work in it, remains the gutter.

And, that night talking film and drinking wine in that low-lit cutting room with John Scott, how I wished to tell him that I had been accidentally blown from the republic of letters into the strange country of film, and, though there was much to despise in the way of chicanery in the world from which I had come, that I had ruefully realised I would rather live in a republic, however flawed, than in a tyranny, no matter how magnificent.

But I could feel the undertow of his world, and I could feel that I was becoming a trader of images, and no longer having words, I opened another bottle, filled our glasses, and said nothing.

Introduction, Richard Flanagan,
The Sound of One Hand Clapping:
the Film Script (2000)

Bread

'I HAVE NO WORDS, my darling, to write this letter that you may never read. I am writing it into empty space,' Nadia Mandelstam wrote in October 1938, the height of Stalin's Terror, to her husband, the great Russian poet Osip Mandelstam. He had disappeared into the Soviet Gulag, never to return.

'Remember the good taste of bread,' she continued, 'when we got it by a miracle and ate it together. Our happy poverty and the poetry you wrote.'

Nadia Mandelstam was to remember not only the taste of bread, but committed to memory all of Osip Mandelstam's poems, carrying in her head what was banned and destroyed and no longer existed in books.

My own memories of bread are not dramatic, but to me they are beautiful. They begin with my mother, from whom I learnt to make bread as a child, for though breadmaking can be learnt from a book, it is best learnt from someone you love.

My mother's family were farming people from Tasmania's north-west coast and my mother gave to all her children a great, abiding love for her land and its people. But it was a special and peculiar love, a love that was about being part of the earth rather than an observer of it.

She would sometimes halt our car full of her six children and our grandmother, a woman of no means and innumerable hatboxes, on the side of a new highway cutting that had sliced open the red earth of the Tasmanian north-west coast, a flick-knife of progress slashing the land. After looking furtively up and down the road, she would get out of the boot old fertiliser bags and order us children to fill them with that rich and sweating red earth.

We would take that dirt all the way back south to our Hobart home, where she would empty it over that part of our backyard wilderness that she decreed would be a vegetable garden, a heroic act of defiance against our suburban plight and domestic dreariness. With her foot she would contemptuously scuff back the surface of some of the sour grey clay of southern Tasmania, and say:

'Soil! Huh! That's not soil, son!'

And then she would put her hands, chapped and dry and cracked from incessant housework, into that wet, heavy red soil, and lift it up in front of us as though it were the most exquisite balm, as if it were an offering to God, and say:

'Smell that, son.'

And we would smell the richness together as she let it fall through her fingers, a shower of red earth, saying:

'Now that's what I call soil.'

And as we spread it about, she would tell me stories about her father, who used to plough his red-earthed fields with two draught horses, and about growing up on a small farm that nestled in the green hills that rise up halfway between the blue immensity of Bass Strait and the blue elegance of Mount Roland, and tell me how her father would each morning walk down the three back steps of his wooden cottage and fall to his knees and thank God for such beauty.

She would tell how she was taught to make bread by her mother on that farm forever mythical in my family's memory; of her mother's stories of having to walk to other farms when, pre-commercial yeast, the yeast plant by accident died.

And then we would go back inside because it was time to knock down and knead the bread dough she made every day.

Earth, flour, dough: all these fell through her knobbly fingers like the life-giving forces they are; she was always half-smeared with flour, a Boadicea of bread-making.

She would take me with her to Gibson's old flour mill to get the 25-pound bags of flour fresh as fresh can be, to smell the dusty flour as we smelt the waxy earth, and she would often have me knead the dough while she went about other work in the kitchen, and sometimes talk wistfully of her Uncle Ding, who had worked for a time at the Sorell bakery before the war, and was a master of the one-handed knead, a concept we sometimes tried to emulate to little avail.

My mother laboured under my father's palate, not so much traditional as convict in its simplicity. When they married in 1947 she prepared him meat and four veg, as she had seen so enticingly prepared in Joan Fox's Launceston boarding house when she had been a young teacher.

My father grew quieter meal by meal, until several weeks into their marriage he pleaded:

'Helen, this modern cooking is all very fine, but can we just get back to meat and two veg?'

Still, ascetic though his tastes were, his palate was not to be underestimated. He was no mug when it came to bread, and recognised old bakers' tricks when a few years ago I left him with a loaf, the leavening of which had been aided with the commercial baker's friend lecithin. On my next visit I knew he had me when he said he didn't agree with the spoiling of good bread with rubbery chemicals.

He taught me how to enjoy bread, with the black pudding he sometimes cooked over the fire for breakfast, or cold muttonbirds and the bread heavily buttered. The smooth comfort of the butter fat, and the gamey stride of the muttonbird fat mingling with the white bread crumbling in your mouth. Or my mother's apricot jam; great gobs of fruit set in a syrup from heaven atop a thick hunk of bread still warm from the oven.

Such passions, however, have lately suffered from the affronts of fashion. Bread is under attack from an ever more obese West desperate to reduce its girth. The Atkins Diet, with its constipating contempt for bread, has had such a profound effect on American diets that it has, according to some reports, led to wheat farmers in the US abandoning wheat for new crops.

What is amusing fad often begets rancorous ideology. An argument is now abroad that man undid himself when he left the hunt for flesh and took to domesticating grain; that the resultant diet destroyed us spiritually and engendered the barbaric exploitation of the modern world that now threatens our very survival.

Such beefsteak enthusiasms were put with muscular clarity by the American Richard Manning in a highly readable essay, 'The Oil We Eat', published in *Harper's*.

Man, according to Manning, has for most of his history gathered and hunted. The recent domestication of grains that marks the invention of agriculture has been a ruinous experiment for both humanity and the planet.

'Agriculture was not so much about food,' Manning writes, 'as it was about the accumulation of wealth. It benefited some people, and those people have been in charge ever since.'

Ten grievous millennia follow, with all the horrors we are too familiar with to bother listing. In this history, rice, corn and wheat are newly inducted to the annals of infamy to sit alongside such old favourites as Attila the Hun and Joseph Stalin.

He ends the essay in a poignantly American manner: by shooting an elk grazing on native grasses near his house.

'Food is politics. This being the case, I voted with my weapon of choice. My particular bit of violence, though, is more satisfying, I think, than the rest of the globe's ordinary political mayhem. I used a rifle to opt out of an insane system.'

Bread, thankfully, isn't politics. It's what people share while suffering politics and what people dream of when politics takes everything from them.

I suppose wallaby and kangaroo are our elk equivalent, and I like my roo, and I like my wallaby chorizo, but I like it balanced with bread of my own making. For me, it is a simple, wonderful thing. My weapon of choice is a bread bowl, preferably porcelain.

Why? Because you need something large, and with weight to balance your kneading, and with thermal mass to keep the dough warm.

But it's not essential. I have made perfectly good bread using a four-litre ice-cream container, and once, at a shack, a plastic bucket.

It has taken me many years to realise how few people actually know how to cook bread. Why this trepidation it is hard to say. Even those I have met who are splendid, highly skilful cooks shy from the prospect of baking. And yet nothing could be simpler.

Reducing bread to its simplest elements will give you the best-tasting bread; for baking is about less, not more. Less rather than more yeast. Less rather than more salt. And no sugar, or raising agents, or, as I read in one recipe, porridge.

None of these is necessary, and if not as harmful as the white lead once used to whiten the loaves of Regency England, they diminish rather than improve the quality of the bread.

Into 500g of plain flour stir with a knife one sachet (7g or one teaspoon) of dried yeast. The fresher the flour, generally, the better. Lately, though, I have baked good loaves using an Italian flour, which is odd, given that it must be some months old by the time I get it.

Make a well in the flour and pour in 300ml of water in which you have dissolved half a teaspoon of salt. The water should be tepid, a vague word that people think means warm, but for the purposes of baking, means not cold. Anything much warmer than not cold runs the risk of killing the yeast.

Next, plunge your hand in and stir it around slowly like it's a dough hook. Gradually fold the flour into the water with your circling fingers. As flour varies in the amount of water it will absorb according to type and age, you may need to add more water.

As the dough forms, aim for an elastic ball with your mix.

When nearly ready, sprinkle a little, but not too much, olive oil over the ball, and work this in. The dough ought to become as roly-poly and cheeky as a baby's bum. It shouldn't feel sludgy or shreddy, but rather should pull cleanly away from the bowl. The dough will feel what it is: alive.

Cover the dough with a tea towel or cling wrap and leave to rise.

Dough will rise in a fridge, albeit very slowly, so you don't need to worry about overheating it. By all means find the bowl a place in the sun or near a heater, but then let it take however long it needs. It will rise.

Be aware that draughts, not cold, kill yeast. Often bowls of bread dough are put in a warm spot also subject to a draught or breeze, and the aspiring baker cannot understand why the dough has failed to rise.

Once risen, either start the second kneading, or punch it down and leave it to rise again, comforted in the knowledge that the longer the rise the better the baked loaf will taste. I like leaving mine overnight and the difference in quality between a four-hour and sixteen-hour rise is startling.

There are many different kneading techniques, but as my grandmother used to tell my elder sister with a gravel of exasperation in her voice—'Stretch the dough, Mary, don't bash it to death.'

Kneading is all about stretching and lengthening the dough. It's not about beating as with a cake, or 'keeping it light' as with scones. Push the base of your palm into the ball of dough and stretch it out as far as it will go. At the end of the stretch, roll the remainder of the ball to the extended end; quarter turn the dough, and stretch the dough again, and so on, until you have a lovely elastic ball.

Knowing when dough is kneaded is most important. If you are not sure, then it's not ready. But suddenly it will develop a spring and tautness and sheen around its skin, and you will know that this is what bread dough should look and feel like.

Shape the loaf as you will, or place in a tin. Leave, covered with a tea towel, to rise a second time.

While writing a novel in Tuscany I had the good fortune to make the acquaintance of a baker, Sandro, the fourth and last generation of his family to be the bakers of the small village of Donnini. I was invited to his birthday party where, after a sumptuous and never-ending series of courses, Sandro sang opera and nineteenth-century chamber music to his friends, dressed for the occasion in a suit like Pavarotti.

In his bakery he showed me the large arch where his forefathers' wood-fired oven used to sit before he replaced it with an electric oven.

His staple was one of the simplest and most delightful of breads, pane Toscana, or Tuscan bread, which is made with only yeast, water and flour, but without salt. The resulting loaves have a great balance of lightness and substance, a lovely crumb, and the lack of salt creates an odd sweet-ness of taste.

Perhaps conditioned by generations of cake cooking, we tend to put our bread in ovens too cool and not leave them there long enough. Unlike a cake, full of sugar and shortening, bread will bake a long time before it burns, and good bread needs to bake a long time.

These days, following the example of Sandro, who replicates the dying fall of a wood-fired oven by starting his baking with intense heat then dropping the temperature, I preheat my oven to 300°C, then place the loaf in, along with a cake tin of hot water. The resulting steam humidifies the oven and helps create a crisper crust.

After five minutes I turn the oven down to 220°C and then keep my eye on the loaf, letting it bake a further 35 minutes.

But all ovens vary. Keep an eye on the bread, and shape your times to your oven and the size of your loaves.

Once cooked, leave to cool for at least an hour. The longer the loaf is left uncut and able to continue slowly cooking the better.

But whenever the loaf is put on the table, few foods will produce such joy in others as when bread appears. A new aroma of delight and fresh memories rise with every slice, and all things—stories, friends and family, food and love and lives—are for a short time as they ought to be: one.

'When people ask what I do,' Sandro told me, 'I tell them I have the most beautiful job in the world. I say: I bake bread.'

The Age
4 October 2005

The History of Love

BOOKS BEGIN FOR ME in very simple ways. Sometimes it's just a picture in which I sense is hidden an entire universe of meaning. When I was about twenty I was poking through a catastrophe of colonial paintings at the back of a Hobart museum with an art curator when I came upon a simple watercolour. I thought it was very beautiful and inexplicably moving. It was a picture of a small Aboriginal girl in a beautiful red silk dress bound with a black velvet band.

It's Mathinna, the curator told me. And he told me the story.

Mathinna was one of the few Aboriginals to have survived the horrors of the Black War in Van Diemen's Land. In 1841, at the age of six, she was adopted by the governor of Van Diemen's

Land, a famous Arctic explorer called Sir John Franklin, and his wife, Lady Jane. She became a black princess, an experiment to show that savages could be raised by education to the level of Europeans. But the experiment failed and she became a sort of exotic pet for the governor and his wife.

When Franklin was recalled to London in 1843, the Franklins abandoned their adopted daughter, dumping her at an orphanage. Subsequently, Mathinna descended into the sorry life of a fringe dweller, caught between grog and prostitution, between a white world that despised her and a despairing black world she despised. At seventeen she was found dead, drowned in a puddle.

And having told me this, the curator detached the old oval frame from the painting.

Look at this, he said.

Cut off at the ankles by the frame were two dark, shoeless feet. Embarrassed by her not wearing shoes, the Franklins had cut Mathinna off at the ankles.

That picture remained with me. More than anything else, those two bare feet haunted me. I'd think about that pretty little girl who wouldn't wear shoes. Years later I spent time in the Kimberley bush with tribal Aboriginals who told me how shoes blinded you from the earth and life, how everything rose up through your feet. And I thought there was a story in those bare feet and that picture, a beautiful story.

But though I tried, I couldn't write that story. Why that was, I can't say. Stories need some leaven, something that takes you into their heart, something that tells you what the blood of that tale is for you. Without that blood moving through it and its teller, the story cannot live.

I stumbled on a history of Sir John Franklin's final folly. After abandoning Mathinna and returning to England, he was appointed to lead the most expensive expedition in British naval history to find the North-West Passage. He and his expedition sailed into the Arctic and promptly vanished. Their fate was the great mystery of the age.

About this I already knew a little. What I didn't know was that nine years later, a polar explorer named Dr Rae returned from the Arctic to London with shocking news gathered from Inuit people he had met. The Franklin expedition were all dead. Worse, at the end, they had taken to eating each other.

The news rocked Britain, Europe and the Empire. Eating people was, after all, what savages did, not great English explorers. Lady Jane Franklin, determined to salvage her husband's name, persuaded no less a figure than Charles Dickens to help.

This led me to reread some of Dickens' work. It became evident to me how strongly Dickens believed that the distance between savagery and civilisation was the capacity to control wanting. He had succeeded in achieving with himself what the Franklins had failed to with Mathinna: disciplining an undisciplined heart. And it was therefore unsurprising that after meeting with Lady Jane, Dickens wrote an article attacking Dr Rae's account, arguing that no civilised man would stoop so low as to resort to cannibalism. For Dickens, the answer was obvious: the Esquimeaux, true savages, had eaten Franklin's men. History was to prove Dr Rae right, but too late to save him from Dickens' attack.

Having triumphed with his article, however, a strange thing happened. Seeing in the image of ice-bound men a mirror image of his own increasingly miserable life, Dickens became obsessed by the story of Franklin. He staged a play about Arctic explorers, which starred his family and friends in supporting parts and him as an Arctic explorer who conquers his passion for a woman in love with another man. It was an unexpected sensation, Dickens' performance stunning. Everyone from Queen Victoria down wanted to see the play, and Dickens reprised it for some charity performances in Manchester.

Because he was now playing a very large theatre he got in a family of professional actresses, the Ternans, to help him. In front of two thousand weeping spectators, the forty-five-year-old Dickens would nobly die each night in front of the eighteen-year-old Ellen Ternan as he declaimed his undying love. His performance was now almost unearthly. Even Ellen Ternan would be overcome and cry uncontrollably.

And at that point Dickens' life changed irrevocably. Caught in the limelight and cradled in the arms of an actress, Charles Dickens fell in love. It was as if the play was a metamorphosis, the role a cocoon out of which a different man emerged.

Within a year he would be separated from his wife, and he and Ellen Ternan would become a couple until his death. The year after his separation, he would reprise the plot of the play—of a man who sacrifices the love of his life for a principle—in a new novel, beginning it with one of the most famous openings in English literature:

It was the best of times, it was the worst of times, it was the age of wisdom, it was the age of foolishness, it was the epoch of belief, it was the epoch of incredulity, it was the season of Light, it was the season of Darkness, it was the spring of hope, it was the winter of despair, we had everything before us, we had nothing before us, we were all going direct to Heaven, we were all going direct the other way . . .

A Tale of Two Cities, as he called the novel, has as its heroine Lucie Mannette, who some critics regard as modelled on Ellen Ternan. It has also been suggested that the novel's two heroes—the base, undisciplined Sydney Carton and virtuous, disciplined Charles Darnay—whose physical similarity is almost perfect, represent two opposing aspects of Dickens' own character. The novel is much concerned with the idea of resurrection.

I saw that the story of Dickens and the story of Mathinna were in some indefinable sense really one: two poles of the same globe. They were joined both by an odd series of events and by the way in which, as human beings, we so often damage ourselves by being untrue to our nature, and yet how being true to our nature is also no guarantee of happiness.

I wished to write about how we try to control our souls, about our terrible need for love, and the cost to our souls when we deny that need. I began the book with an unknown Aboriginal girl running barefoot through the wet kangaroo grass of an island at the edge of the world, and ended it twenty years later, with the most famous man of his time at the centre of the world, feeling tears raining down on him, a man who believed wanting could be controlled by reason, finally realising that reason is a fine thing, but wanting is the very essence of life.

And writing these words, I wonder if the history of love is this: a terrible war waged between bare feet and wooden frames that never ends.

Afterword, Richard Flanagan,
Wanting (2008)

Louder Than the Storm

I FIRST MET Vlado Kreslin in the late European summer of '99, in a hot back street in the old town of Ljubljana. In the late summer there can be few lovelier cities in Europe, and we walked to a café through its ochre-coloured Hapsburg streets, along its somnolent river, past the smell of its teeming cafés and bars, so many serene images at odds with those normally presented of this troubled part of the world.

I had heard Vlado Kreslin's music, a magic fusion of so many Mitteleuropean motifs, that put me in mind of everything from the films of Emir Kusturica to the novels of Bohumil Hrabal. I was conscious of his reputation as Slovenia's most feted musician, a singer-songwriter whose hits over two decades have spanned everything from traditional tunes to a recent song for the Slovene soccer team; a musician of such standing that everyone who comes to central Europe—from Dylan to REM—plays with him, and which saw our every conversation punctuated by requests for his autograph.

His dress that day, if somewhat curious, managed to be both impeccably traditional and entirely unconventional, a sleight of hand he pulled off in his music as well. In a city highly conscious of how it looked, where everyone wore tasteful tonal shades of blue and grey, he wore green, an outfit that to my alien eyes looked like that of an Austro–Hapsburg gamekeeper, circa 1914.

He was tall, but seemed taller, and was ebullient and outgoing, exuberant and warm. He slapped me on the back with vigour repeatedly, told stories incessantly: amusing, droll and punctuated with a great braying laugh.

But every now and then he would lean low and interrupt the river of his talk with a single sentence that was direct and pointed, a conspiratorial aside, practised, one felt, through a life growing up in a less than free society. His songs were not dissimilar—exotic and delightful, yet hidden away in them the unexpected kernel of some greater meaning.

I had that day returned from Belgrade, still reeling from the war that had concluded only a few short weeks earlier, and with Vlado was going to a concert in the industrial town of Celje.

Along with a great deal of poverty, distress and fear, I met in Belgrade a Serbian Orthodox priest in a bar who, it transpired, was a mad keen Celtic supporter. He drank black beer, and every second or third glass would reach into his bag, pull out and don the famous green and white striped jersey, then sing the Celtic team song. Though with his long raven black hair and beard he looked for all the world like an archetypal Serb, his mother was Croatian and he had recently been beaten up by some local Serbs.

Over the next few days, he introduced me to fellow members of his band, the Belgrade Craic, an Irish folk band of the Pogues type. They all had assumed names such as Danny O'Leary and Brigid O'Donohue, though their real names were of the order of Bogdan Bogdanovic. Their ambition was to become an internationally successful Irish folk band. In Belgrade in the late summer of '99, there were worse imaginable futures.

Through Danny and Brigid I discovered the bizarre Celtic sub-culture of Belgrade, where bands such as Orthodox Celts reigned supreme, and people took Irish trips to Prague, which, I was assured, had the best Irish pubs in central Europe. On a visit to London the Serbian Orthodox priest had even spat on Cromwell's statue, only to be hit by his girlfriend and told not to behave like a peasant. When I asked why they identified with the Irish, I was told that the Serbs, like the Irish, were victims.

One night in a Belgrade bar, after several rounds of 'Dirty Old Town', the Belgrade Craic launched into some singing in their own tongue. Upon asking what these songs were, I was told that they were traditional Serbian Kosovar songs. And then, as one, the Belgrade Craic cracked glasses together and roared in English, 'Serbia is Kosovo! Kosovo is Serbia!'

I left on the train for Slovenia the following morning. In the same distance it would take to travel between Sydney and Melbourne, I passed through three countries and an unceasing rhythm of white buildings broken and blackened by war.

That evening, as I drove with Vlado Kreslin along narrow alpine roads to Celje, I thought how, for all its extreme horror, Belgrade seemed only the new Europe in extreme, ever more nationalistic, its borders closing down all difference, its remnant people lost. Vlado Kreslin's music seemed to be about something else.

If Vlado Kreslin wasn't what one expected of central Europe, nor was Slovenia, a small, mostly snowcapped alpine land of beauty that sits like a pearl between the great shells of Italy and Austria to one side, and Hungary and Croatia to the other. It is, writes Claudio Magris, the great chronicler of Mitteleuropa and its decline, the last genuine Austro–Hapsburg landscape.

It is also a fascinating country that has improbably emerged from the fall of Communism as one of the more successful new nations of Europe. With a population of fewer than two million, its traditions have long been liberal, and its national heroes are not warriors but the poets whose images adorn their numerous brands of spirits. Yet Slovenia can sometimes seem hopelessly confused culturally.

Desperate to free itself from what it sees as the terrible shame of the Balkans, its high culture often seems intent upon complete identification with the West. So much that is fascinating about Slovenia, however, arises from it belonging to both East and West, neither alone defining or explaining this fecund country's riches.

In such a world, torn between the East and the West, the past and the future, Vlado Kreslin's lively melodies and moody lyrics about the natural world of the Pannonian flatlands, the storks and the bees and the Mura River; his Bosnian songs and Gypsy influences, sung in a strong dialect obscure even to his own countrymen, are resented by some of the cultural elite as not truly Slovenian. In a Europe where Gypsies remain despised and oppressed, his very first hit song, 'Old Black Guitar', was about how as a child Gypsies would visit their home and play music with his father.

I had heard criticism of Vlado Kreslin, and perhaps less than surprisingly it came from Slovenian high artists who saw his work as not 'pure' Slovene, and who felt his decision to sing Bosnian songs (which they described as Turkish), to include Gypsy elements in his music, was a betrayal of the artist's mission to create a true and pure national art.

But then Vlado Kreslin was born an outsider, in the remote region of Prekmurje. Until 1919, when it was formally hived off from the old Empire as part of the Versailles settlement and given to the new nation of Yugoslavia, Prekmurje was part of Hungary.

Though the majority of its people were Slovene, Prekmurje was the antithesis of Slovenia. Instead of great alps and verdant green valleys, it was a part of the great muddy plain of Pannonia. Its Slovenes were Protestant, rather than Catholic; its population diverse, not homogenous, with Hungarian, Gypsy, German and, until the Holocaust, a substantial Jewish population. Even its cuisine is different; and to this day, its dialect remains difficult for other Slovenes to follow.

When in the late 1980s Slovenia's path began to diverge from that of Yugoslavia's, so too did Vlado Kreslin's from that of the more conventional singer-songwriter that he had up until that point been. As Milosevic rose to power in Belgrade on a platform of Greater Serbia, beginning with a campaign against Albanian Kosovars, the Slovenes led the fight for a more democratic, freer Yugoslavia. The Slovene Spring, as it was known, was a ferment that found manifold expression, including the rise of the Slovenian Green movement founded and led by Vlado Kreslin's best friend, Stefan Smej, until his untimely death of cancer.

It was Smej who at this time encouraged Vlado Kreslin to form a new band with some of the oldest inhabitants of his home village of Beltinska, playing a blend of traditional and contemporary music.

The Beltinska Banda, as they became known, were a Mitteleuropean Buena Vista Social Club. As Yugoslavia fell apart in a series of bloody wars, these dozen or sometimes more traditional musicians (including Vlado's own mother and father) aged from their late sixties to their early nineties took to the stage in black suits and black homburgs, playing everything from traditional tunes to Vlado

Kreslin's own songs through to standards as diverse as 'Summertime' and Iggy Pop's 'Passenger', and became a national institution.

At Celje, at the soccer field where the concert was to be played, I met the Beltinska Banda—including Vlado's mother and father—behind the stage, and was shown the venerable, battered instruments they played.

Later, watching the concert, I found their music by turns wistful, melancholic and moving, and running through the songs that night so much of Kreslin himself: a certain joyousness coupled to an ache that seemed autumnal, through which swirled the gypsy sounds of the dulcimer and fiddle and accordion.

Up the front were Bosnian and Serbian teen-agers in Metallica T-shirts, while down the back were people who may well have been their grand-parents. Dark clouds gathered around the cooling towers of the Celje power plant and it began to rain, but the singing of the crowd only grew louder, their dancing that encompassed the front third of the crowd only more determined.

I thought how so much of great modern art and writing had arisen out of the old polyglot world of central Europe, with its Jewish and Islamic influences, with its wash of so many different peoples. I thought of how growing up in the shadow of White Australia, Europe and its ceaseless diversity had been so attractive, yet how now it was we who had become diverse and Europe that had become so many little white Australias, enclaves of pure ethnicity of one variety or another.

As I looked around Vlado Kreslin's audience— the Serbian workers and their families, the young Bosnians, as well as the Slovenes—I realised that Vlado Kreslin's music was at once entirely of his world and yet enlarged that world to include anyone else who wished to be part of it.

His music spoke to a notion of a better, more generous world than that coming into being in the charred ruins of Vukovar and Srebrenica and Pristina, that cracked horror seeking identity with spurious notions of victimhood and Pogues songs that I had met with in Belgrade. In an era of ever narrower nationalisms, it suggested a broader humanity, a more generous idea both of culture and of people, and it did it with an exquisite music rooted in the polyglot traditions of a world that is elsewhere being forcibly dismantled.

And, in a soccer field that evening in the late summer of Europe, such things seemed not unimportant. At the front of the audience, Vlado's father had got down from the stage and was dancing in the rain and mud of the mosh pit with the teenagers. At the back of the concert, seeking refuge with me in a team shelter, was a woman holding a baby who had begun singing along with Vlado on stage.

'We remember a song which once belonged to us all,' she sang softly in a Serbian accent, mouth close to her baby's ear, 'when our laughter was louder than the roar of the storm.'

The Age
30 December 2000

Family Is Everything

IT WAS A LAND of fear and uncertainty and gas masks selling out in the Blue Mountains and anthrax scares in Darwin. It was an election no one cared less about because no one any longer felt any connection to either party and its apparatchik parroting focus group polling parroting doorstops and five second grabs parroting shock jock denunciations. It was a vortex of meaningless nonsense, occasionally seasoned with a racist overtone to give it the semblance if not the reality of veracity. It was the season for charlatans, a time of lies and hate sold as a righteous fear. It was the Australian Federal Election of 2001.

Yet in the end the most haunting image the election threw up was not that of a presidential Howard embracing world leaders or an avuncular Beazley embracing punters. Rather, it was a picture of three smiling young girls, three girls who looked radiant, beautiful children, who drowned along with some 350 other refugees falsely hopeful of becoming Australians after their boat sank.

In the end it was a vile time to live through and a vile place to be, this nation that once seemed so generous and open, and it happened because finally it was once more all right to do and say such things because the people who were going to suffer were wogs, and wogs were what we once more no longer wanted with their diseases and their violence and their closet horrors.

Because in the end, of course, it wasn't so much a national election as a national disgrace, in which our two major parties did not so much play the race card, as back it to the hilt with cracked rhetoric about the integrity and defence of borders that sounded eerily reminiscent of the arguments that built in Weimar Germany of threatened living space.

The ALP had long ago established that its venality and chicanery were beyond doubt, but this callousness without care for the consequences was new and horrifying.

Labor tried to pretend it was about domestic issues. But the only job they were after was a job for the big puffy boy who, with his one great ironical gift, that of diminishment, managed to make a national election sound like a botched pitch for the job of assistant manager of a bottle shop. He was qualified all right, he and his mates, conceited bastards all born to rule as much as those they derided on the government benches; the only health they cared for, that of their pirates' fortunes depicted in the polling charts; the only education they knew, the re-education of any who dissented with a line that now so resembled the Liberals that only girth and eyebrows could be used to distinguish foe from friend.

There was no doubt that the times were weirdly out of joint. In the ALP, senior figures would say in private that Kim's words were just Kim's strategy, that in victory a new generosity would emerge. But in public they said nothing, and the moral torpor that has so long affected the party shaded into a larger and unforgiveable cowardice. Public men have to be judged by public actions, and Beazley drifted through the election like a lost blimp in search of a guiding breeze.

In Sydney the film of the moment was a meditation on trust and betrayal. Called *Lantana*, it posed the question of whether trust betrayed can ever be made whole again.

In a room in that same city a father refused water because every time he drank it reminded him of the mouths of his three beautiful daughters filling with water, irrevocably, fatally. The man had a name: Ahmed Alzalimi. His dead daughters had names: Eman, eight years old, Zahra, six years old, and Fatimah, five years old. He had a wife whose father was killed by Saddam Hussein's secret police when she was five. She survived the sinking and was taken back to Indonesia. And she too had a name: Sondos Ismael.

The media told us Kim Beazley was a good man. But like John Howard, Kim Beazley did not think this man ought to be allowed to breach the conditions of his temporary protection visa by travelling to Indonesia to be with his grieving wife. Rules were rules.

This is not my Australia, I wanted to say to that grieving father. I wanted to tell him things that were not possible: how if I could sing the sea out of his sweet daughters' lungs and have them Australian, oh how I would have. To say that I was ashamed and lost and my country with me and no one any longer knew the way back from such terrible shame, this shame that was now ours.

But words were cheaper than children's lives in Australia now, and all were relaxed and comfortable inside their lounge rooms, curtains firmly drawn, and no one wished to venture outside to see the corpses that flecked the distant ocean like storm-tossed kelp leaves.

The Age
9 November 2001

Postscript

On 3 December 2006, minutes after the ALP caucus had replaced him as leader with Kevin Rudd, Kim Beazley was told that his younger brother had unexpectedly died. His brother had a name: David.

At a press conference held shortly after, Kim Beazley was reported to have blinked back tears when he said, 'Family is everything.'

Our Keith

I FIRST MET Akif Lutfiu on a wintry Hobart night. The rendezvous was appropriately clandestine, arranged after a series of meetings with intermediaries, phone calls being considered too dangerous following previous Australian Federal Police raids.

Snow was falling on the mountain above the house in which we filmed a two-hour interview that we hoped might form the basis of a documentary about this enigmatic fugitive.

The story of how Akif Lutfiu, Kosovar refugee, fugitive and soon to be deportee, had become Our Keith, a cause célèbre in Tasmania, intrigued me. He was, as one caller to radio commented, a bushranger for our times, but his story was also something else—that of two communities seeking to regain a lost dignity, and of two nations that seemed to have lost their way in the world.

Akif Lutfiu's appearance was as much a surprise as his character. He was good-looking and dressed in fashionable street wear, more one's idea of a New York Latino rapper than an Albanian Muslim. He had in consequence an odd presence.

He was frustrating to interview, because his personality was as unexpected as his looks. Nothing about him fitted any preconceptions. His short life was an almost absurdly neat fit with the last torturous twenty years of Kosovar history, yet none of this overly interested Akif Lutfiu. He had stock positions about the Serbs, but his heart seemed not so much in stock denunciations as it had been with the Serbian girls with whom he had once gone out.

He seemed to know little about his nation's history and politics, beyond a determination not to be their victim. He was nevertheless fiercely Albanian and Muslim, and angry at what that meant his fate would be.

He seemed to have little perspective on his life, as though he still lived in the shadow of the enormity of all that had befallen him. His stories were muddled and imprecise, and, one suspected, sometimes exaggerated. There was about him an undeniable sadness.

Born in 1980, orphaned at the age of fifteen, he appears to have become a street kid, and lived for periods of time as an illegal immigrant in Turkey and Italy. By 1999 he was back living with his cousins in Pristina, listening to rap, the musical choice of young Albanians. The Serbs, he said, preferred techno.

His exile from his homeland began in a Serbian roundup of Pristina residents on 1 April 1999. His description of that event has chilling parallels with other round-ups in ghettos in other times.

According to Akif Lutfiu's account, JNA soldiers went through the streets calling through a megaphone upon residents to leave or be killed. Pristina, he said, was like a hell.

He recalled joining a great river of people being forced to the railway station. Bodies lay dead or dying on the road, shot or beaten. To look down or halt to help was to risk the same fate. In the crush of people at the railway station a woman handed him a baby and asked him to look after it while she found her other children. The baby was dead.

Akif Lutfiu spent a month in a refugee camp in Macedonia, and then, though wishing to go to Germany or Sweden, he ended up coming to Australia, one of four thousand Kosovar refugees belatedly admitted into Australia by the Howard Government. When accepted for Australia he was unsure even as to what language was spoken here.

Four hundred of these Kosovars were sent on to Tasmania and settled at the old Brighton Army camp on the outskirts of Hobart's northern suburbs. The Brighton camp abuts the housing commission suburbs of Bridgewater and Gagebrook. Outside of Aboriginal settlements, according to Anglicare, these are some of the most deprived and impoverished areas in Australia.

It might have been expected that Tasmanians would ignore, or even grow hostile to, the government-sponsored refugees, given how the island is routinely portrayed as redneck and reactionary. Yet when one beleaguered community looked into the eyes of another worse off, it perhaps saw something familiar. The response from ordinary Tasmanians was, according to Stefano Lufi, one of three Albanians living in Hobart, 'utterly extraordinary'.

The Brighton Kosovars were flooded with offers of help and gestures of friendship. Businesses provided them with free clothes, free food, free meals, free tours. Cinemas gave them free weekly tickets. The state Labor Government became strong supporters, as did the local Brighton council. The Hobart newspaper, *The Mercury*, ran articles in Albanian. A commercial television news broadcast began with an introduction in Albanian. Far from being outcast, the Kosovars were taken in.

At first Akif Lutfiu, who had not properly washed since he left Pristina, spent hours standing under hot showers at the camp. Then he began to make friends in Hobart, started to work, started to buy things and went dancing every Saturday night in local clubs.

When Akif Lutfiu says he fell in love with Tasmania it is difficult not to believe him. In Kosovo he had carried a gun. In Kosovo he was bound by the obligations of the blood feud. In Kosovo difference demanded conflict. Akif Lutfiu was unprepared for what he found in Tasmania. 'Here in Tasmania, I am with twelve people, everyone different, different religion, different faith, it doesn't matter. I have Chinese friends, Japanese, Filipino, Italian, Bosnian, Croatian. Everyone I have here. Everyone different language. Everyone is Christian, Catholic, Buddhist, Muslim. Everyone is one man.' His Tasmanian friends called him Keith. He called himself 'a Tassie boy'.

'My heart will stay here in Tasmania,' Akif Lutfiu told me that night as snow fell low on the mountain above us, 'they can only take my body back.'

He wanted to live his life in Tasmania. His dream was to get work, a car licence, go to TAFE and learn computers and pay back his friends their generosity. He never thought the Australian government would force him or other Kosovars to go back.

His life shaped by the evil of idiotic nationalisms, he refused to be defined by any idea of national sovereignty. From Akif Lutfiu's point of view every white person in Australia was, as he put it, 'an illegal tourist'. For that reason he didn't understand why John Howard wouldn't say sorry.

'You're in their land and you don't say sorry—come on, man.'

He wished he had been born five hundred years ago and could travel anywhere he wished.

'I am a man of the earth,' he said. 'I was born on the earth. I was not born in Mars or Jupiter. I can live everywhere in the world. I am a man. I am a man, I have hands. I am not evil. I can live anywhere.'

But then in April of this year the Federal Government made clear its intent to repatriate all refugees to Kosovo and Akif Lutfiu was no longer a man of the earth but, as so many of his people have been over the last millennium, an Albanian on the run.

'That make me very, very sad,' Akif Lutfiu said. 'I feel like I am running from the Serbs. I feel like someone can kill me. And in my heart you know what I feel? That I can kill myself.'

At dawn of 2 May 2000, armed federal police raided the Colebrook home of Colin Parramore, a bus driver who had worked at the Kosovar refugee haven at Brighton. Wearing bullet-proof vests they broke locks on sheds and turned the house over searching for Akif Lutfiu.

But Akif Lutfiu had left the day before. He was now a haunted as well as hunted man. His dreams altered. On the run he dreamt of being caught by immigration officers, and that he would push and push them to make them shoot him, and that then, dead, he would finally be free.

The raid made front-page news in Tasmania. The public mood, which had been highly pro-Albanian, now swung solidly behind Lutfiu.

The following month Tony Foster, the mayor of Brighton, the municipality that covers the working-class suburbs of Bridgewater and Gagebrook, returned from visiting Kosovo with Tasmanian Albanian Ray Duraj. At his own expense, Foster had visited as many of the Brighton Kosovars as possible, and set up a sister-city relationship between Brighton and Ferizaj, a city of 130,000 people. What he found was many of the former Brighton Kosovars living in what he described as impossible situations.

'I have never before felt so ashamed to be Australian,' he said on his return. 'How could we send people back to this?' He found former Brighton Kosovars such as Refik Zuzaju contemplating suicide. 'I think I might go up to a high bridge,' said Zuzaju. 'We have no future.' Zuzaju's thirteen-year-old daughter, Valbona, clung to

Ray Duraj's arm when the two left, sobbing and crying, begging him, 'to put her in his pocket and take her back to Tasmania'. Foster was so upset he vomited shortly after leaving.

Foster found families whose children had played with his, with no money, no jobs and no homes, living in tents or squalid, unfurnished rooms, families in transit centres where the only food supplied was rice and spaghetti, and showers were allowed only once a week.

And Tony Foster found that the Kosovars had not forgotten Tasmania.

'It was almost embarrassing the way people begged us, day after day, to tell everyone how much they appreciated what Tasmania and Tasmanians had done for them.'

Foster's comments were prominently reported and made a deep impression on many in Tasmania, and heightened the sense that Akif Lutfiu was being unfairly persecuted. Public comments from friends that the fugitive—who now spent his days in safe houses watching television and playing computer games—was deeply depressed and that they feared for his wellbeing, only fuelled this sentiment.

In Hobart's Gatecrasher nightclub, at two o'clock on a Sunday morning, ninety-nine days after he went on the run to avoid being deported back to Kosovo, Akif Lutfiu was arrested by four police officers. For the second time since he had been on the run, he had taken the risk of going out to a bar. The fugitive made a run for it, but was grabbed and held at the door by a bouncer until the police were able to secure him with handcuffs.

Following his arrest, Akif Lutfiu says he was stripped and left naked in a Hobart cell on a cold winter's night, shivering and crying and feeling, he said, 'like a mad, mad dog'.

In a state that is losing one thousand people every year, the one man who had declared a determination to stay was hunted down like a dog by armed police with orders to arrest and deport him.

His arrest once more sparked front-page stories and lead items on television news. The feeling on the part of most Tasmanians appeared to be one of anger tempered by a shame that this had happened in their own community. A television phone-in poll showed 68 per cent of respondents believed the fugitive should be allowed to stay. The acting premier, Paul Lennon, weighed into the fray promising that the Tasmanian government would consider backing legal action in support of Akif Lutfiu. Stefano Lufi's family store filled with strangers offering money for Akif Lutfiu's legal costs.

Commenting on Lutfiu's probable fate, Brighton mayor Tony Foster said that he would in all likelihood be begging in the streets of Pristina within a few days of his return.

Why could we not take those of the Kosovar refugees who wished to make a life here? Why does Australia, unlike the United States and Canada, do such a thing to these people? Why can we not organise our affairs such that places that want more people, such as Tasmania, and the people who wish to live there, such as the Kosovars, be allowed to make common cause?

For a moment, Akif Lutfiu became a symbol for something much larger than his own sorry tale. In his plight a battling community saw the chance to assert a fundamental humanity that no longer is deemed of value or significance. He came to stand for an idea of an Australia that was open, generous and good, an idea for which there is no longer political voice on either side of national politics.

How could he have known that the country that he had found so tolerant and friendly, so large and so generous, in which he so wished to make his life was shrinking before his eyes into something so small and pinched, so uncaring and mean-spirited?

When last I spoke by phone with Akif Lutfiu he was in the Maribyrnong Detention Centre. He was, as ever, mildly precocious, and complained about the way he had been given only cordial to drink, but not Coca-Cola.

'I need Coke, man,' he said. 'I feel sick. I have stress. It is good for my stomach, Coke. Feel bad. Coke, you know it?'

I had forgotten how the story of Akif Lutfiu was now so much bigger than Akif Lutfiu; that he was only an orphaned child soon to be sent back to a country on the brink of collapsing into its old patterns of violence, a spiral of revenge and hatred that, for a short time, Akif Lutfiu had the vanity of thinking he might be allowed to escape.

Five hundred years after he wished to be born, the man of the earth was to return to being a victim of history.

The Age
22 July 2000

Metamorphoses

THIS IS A TALE ABOUT LOVE and change in the heart-shaped island that lies far to your south, and it ought to perhaps begin with that island, which most Australians presume they know, but about which they mostly know nothing.

Tasmania is a state of the much trumpeted federation, but you don't have to sit long at a battered bar in Hobart, say, or wander far into its clearfell-scarred heart, or stand for more than a moment beneath a ninety-metre-high regnans awaiting chainsawing in the Styx Valley of the Giants, to realise this is also another country, and it was to this other country that a troubled young man with a penchant for snappy suits came to work as a doctor in 1972.

The doctor had an affinity with the odd

individuality of places unknown to others; after all, as a teenager in Armidale hadn't he carried a sticker calling for New England to be a state separate of New South Wales? He also had desires that might be unfairly termed political, but were perhaps more those of a young man with an excessive sense of duty: he had been an admirer of Menzies and royalty, and his contemplation of a future career as a Liberal politician had got him as far as the front door of that party's Sydney office in order to join up, only to find the office closed for the day. But a larger sense of confusion and uncertainty as to who he was, and what he might be, meant he never returned.

These confusions were many and not easily, perhaps not possibly, reduced to any single matter. There was the matter of career, which as a doctor in the 1970s ought simply to have meant an acceptance of privilege and wealth, but which somehow didn't satisfy him. There was the matter of his sexuality, which saw him voluntarily submit to electro-shock treatment to rid himself of the desire he felt for men. And there was a passion to identify with something larger than himself, other than himself, a project of self-abnegation that sometimes looked like self-loathing.

Once in Tasmania he began the first of a number of metamorphoses, setting out on various missions, the best word for which is perhaps quixotic.

He spent all his savings paying for an advertisement in national papers. Headlined 'Tasmania—World Epitome of Man's Destructiveness', it detailed the disgraces of the island's history from the Black War through to Lake Pedder. There was a search for the thylacine that turned up only emaciated greyhounds, and an impassioned letter in the wake of the international crisis precipitated by the 1973 Yom Kippur war to editors of all the world's major newspapers, from *Pravda* to the *New York Times* to the *Launceston Examiner*, calling for 'a revolution in human awareness'. 'The only means of this saving grace,' wrote the doctor, 'lies with the individual.' The letter went, unremarkably, unpublished.

When the nuclear aircraft carrier USS *Enterprise* came to Hobart he went and sat on top of Mount Wellington in hail and snow, fasting till the ship moored far below in the Derwent departed, a protest nearly sabotaged by a cousin who poked a cheese sandwich into his tent. Unlike his letter, the doctor's unusual action, which combined landscape, passion and non-violent protest in a highly theatrical gesture, attracted national attention.

What next happened is conventionally told as a tale of a near-mystical journey into the wilderness, of how while rafting the little known Franklin River in 1976, he was inspired to his passionate

leadership and consequent fame as the personi-
fication of the battle to save that same river from
destruction, the man known as Bob Brown.

But Bob Brown had already been changed by
the people he met in Tasmania, most particularly
those conservationists clustered around the world's
first Green party, the United Tasmania Group
(UTG), formed in 1972 to save Lake Pedder.
Even then, the Tasmanian Green movement was
the most dynamic and radical in the country.

It is not possible to understand Brown without
understanding the UTG. In Tasmania the environment movement was never just a battle for
this or that piece of dirt. Rather, each issue
from Pedder onwards, as the poet Pete Hay has
observed, was a prism through which the invisible
light of a century and a half of hope and despair
of a people was refracted into a glorious rainbow
of future possibilities. At its beginning the Green
movement was about the search of the withered
soul of Tasmania for redemption.

While much has been made in the media of
how the Greens have finally gone beyond being a
pack of hippy tree huggers, the reality is that they
never were, and the Australian Greens now in so
many ways represent a full turning of the circle
back to the New Ethic of the UTG, the world's
first coherent Green manifesto that was social and
political as much as it was environmental, and

which made such an impact on the young doctor from New South Wales.

'Finding the UTG,' Brown has written, 'was, for me, like being let out of the prison of conventional thinking.' Brown stood unsuccessfully as a UTG senate candidate in 1975, garnering only 182 votes, and even more unsuccessfully for the Tasmanian parliament in 1976, when he gained only 13 votes.

Though he forgot to vote for himself, he never forgot watching from the gallery of the Tasmanian parliament as both sides of politics voted to flood Pedder, and his belief that the environment needed its own party never thereafter left him. Those who are constantly surprised at his effectiveness as a politician forget how long he has been playing the game, how unlike many mainland environmental groups the Tasmanian Greens never fudged the issue of power. For them, for him, in spite of all the dilemmas it represents, acquiring power is how you change the world. There are no other choices.

By 1976 he was living in a little weatherboard cottage at Liffey beneath Drys Bluff, the snappy doctor now Don Quixote dressed in a new motley of old trousers, heavy boots, open-necked shirts and jumpers. The new environmental battleground was the remaining undammed reaches of the Gordon River and its tributaries—the Jane,

Denison and, most portentously, the Franklin rivers of south-west Tasmania.

At a weekend meeting at Brown's Liffey cottage, a new group was formed with a much smaller ambition than the UTG. Rather than save the world, the Tasmanian Wilderness Society (TWS) aimed only to save what remained of the south-west Tasmanian wilderness. Brown began metamorphosing a second time into the Gandhi of the Rivers, Australian of the Year, Saint Bob of the Wilderness.

The Franklin campaign changed Tasmania, brought the ALP to power federally, and was the beginning of a golden period for the Greens. Never forgetting the lessons of the UTG, Brown spent the 1980s transforming the successes of a pressure group into a broad-based political party, slowly building up a Tasmanian green organisation and its parliamentary representation, culminating in the Greens scoring 18 per cent of the vote in Tasmania at the 1989 state elections and winning the balance of power, becoming the first red–green alliance to govern outside of Germany. His focus was as much international as local, and he built close friendships with the likes of Ralph Nader, David Suzuki and Petra Kelly.

But following the collapse of the Tasmanian Labor–Green Accord in the early 1990s, the withering of federal ALP support for environmental issues, the rise of Howard, the increasingly effective combination of anti-Green propaganda and new legislation that saw forestry protesters fined thousands of dollars or imprisoned for months, the Green movement, not always helped by its own arrogance and self-aggrandisement, experienced defeat and collapse. An attempt to merge the disparate Green groups around the nation with the Democrats to form a national Green party failed. Internationally, the early promise of the Greens similarly faded. Brown's close friend, Petra Kelly, one-time hero of the German Greens, died tragically, her body not found for several days.

Brown had publicly declared himself gay in 1976, but during the years of the Franklin battle he was often portrayed as an asexual ascetic, a monastic figure who existed beyond physical needs and who sublimated his desires in a passion for wilderness.

But however much the issue of Brown's sexuality was pushed away by his supporters, it was brought to the fore by his opponents. In the wake of the Greens' triumph in the 1989 Tasmanian elections, a ferocious anti-gay movement was created by far right groups in Tasmania's depressed north-west, given succour by some Liberal politicians. The real target, of course, was not gays, but the Greens, seeking to destroy the character of their leader Brown.

The attack had unexpected consequences. Some young Tasmanian gay activists led by Rodney Croome and Nick Toonen filled a bus and went to the anti-gay rallies, showing courage not dissimilar to that of the freedom rides of the civil rights battles.

Their hero and model was Bob Brown. As a teenager, Croome had bought Peter Thompson's 1984 biography of Brown, in order, he says, to read over and over the two paragraphs that said he was gay. He hid the book at the back of his bookshelf in his Devonport home.

For such young gays, Brown showed them how it was possible to be both Tasmanian and gay, an identity perhaps best summed up in a bumper sticker of the time: 'We're here, we're queer, and we're not going to the mainland.' Brown advised them on tactics, showed Rodney Croome how to write his first press release, but refused to be publicly drawn too closely into the battle, worrying that it might detract from their efforts, worried also that it might detract from his environmental battles, a decision he now wonders was right or not.

Through the early 1990s the Tasmanian gays fought a long, difficult battle, their campaign modelled on that of the Greens' traditional campaigns in Tasmania, taking the issue of gay rights first to state, then national and finally international forums for resolution.

Brown feels he owes them a great debt. Because of them he was finally able to publicly acknowledge his sexuality as integral rather than separate and subordinate to his political struggles, as he had argued in the 1980s. And perhaps it is because of them that in 1996, at the age of fifty-one, he found what he had evaded yet yearned for all his adult life: a man with whom he could live.

In a backroom full of light above his Tibetan rug shop in central Hobart, I meet Bob Brown's now long-time partner, Paul Thomas. A shy yet genial and open man, he shares similarities of character as well as similarities of upbringing with Bob Brown: a country childhood in the Huon Valley south of Hobart in a religious family—his Catholic, Brown's Presbyterian.

Paul Thomas talks of Bob Brown's closeness to his twin sister and two brothers, of his generosity, giving anyone and everyone whatever he has, a generosity that sees strangers come up and thank him for gifts of money made ten years or more before. He and Brown have been together since, in Paul Thomas' words, they took a walk together on the eve of Brown's return to politics, his election as a Tasmanian senator in the 1996 election.

Since that time Brown's concerns have grown. Though environmental issues continued to loom large, he was the first federal parliamentarian to

continually speak out against mandatory sentenc-
ing, and he argued strongly on other social issues
such as public education and civil liberties that the
ALP were abandoning in their race to outcompete
the Liberals as true conservatives. In the manner
he had built a Tasmanian Green Party in the
1980s he now also set out to build a cohesive and
electorally successful Australian Green party, the
consequences of which are only now beginning to
be apparent.

Four days after the federal election that saw
the Australian Greens emerge as a significant new
force in Australian politics, I visit Bob Brown. I
find the man described as the new leader of the
opposition looking exhausted, his long face heavily
lined. I tell him how I have been given thirty-six
hours to write a large piece on him, and that I am
feeling seasick from gazing out over the ocean of
such a storm-tossed life.

Imagine how I feel, he says, and we both laugh
about that and then about many other things. I
have no idea how you are meant to conduct an
interview, particularly with someone you have
known off and on for twenty years, so instead we
simply swap stories.

He laughs a great deal, and says laughter is
the greatest strength an activist can have. But he
has also the courage that has endured beatings,
imprisonment, bullets in the post, and the less

obvious but perhaps more corrosive horror of ongoing hatred: of his politics and his sexuality.

Like all people described as charismatic, Bob Brown is in the flesh reassuringly ordinary in presence and manner. The son of a policeman who grew up in country New South Wales, Bob Brown has about him many of those paradoxes sometimes called old Australia: a coupling of genuine warmth and a polite reserve; a laconic manner and broad accent that some find gauche and others charming; a country slowness in conversation; a notorious vagueness of language that disguises a quick and sharp mind.

He has what Les Murray in a famous poem about fellow country New South Welshmen defined as sprawl: an elusive largeness of spirit that finds its expression not so much in words but in actions. Both his mother and father came to Bob's Liffey home to die, nursed through the twilight of their lives in the lee of the great Western Tiers by their son.

Our talk veers to politics, of how the Greens seem to have taken over the vast field of the left, abandoned as suddenly and unexpectedly by the ALP as the Taliban fleeing Kabul by night. The Greens' rhetoric has altered: the rights of refugees, the needs of public education, the plight of the poor all rate as significantly as traditional environmental issues. Heroic figures of the old

ALP, such as Tom Uren, came and campaigned for Brown during the election.

The public image of Saint Bob, the serene mystic, does no justice to his considerable gifts as a politician, and is a burden for a man only too conscious of his failings. Revered by some, he is despised by others, even some within the Green movement. There are many who hate Bob Brown, in part because they feel the distance between the public image of Saint Bob and the reality of Bob Brown—the country copper's son willing to fight as hard and tough as his opponents for what he believes in—bespeaks a great hypocrisy.

Having myself brushed up against his more ruthless edges in the past, I put it to him that he is hard in getting what he wants.

'Yes, I am,' he says, without qualification or explanation.

We talk of Olegas Truchanas' famous observation that Tasmania could be a shining beacon, and he reflects that yes, in the last election the refugee issue had no purchase in Tasmania, where sympathy for their plight was high, how not only did the Green vote go spectacularly up, but the Liberal vote went down; that the island, once mocked for its homophobes and rednecks, had become a bastion of reason and compassion in Australia. 'I would like to see the world become Tasmania,' he says.

More stories follow about so many people, and Bob Brown tells me how he has come to realise that humanity is everything, that if we can just find the way to look after ourselves, the environment will be fine.

'People are the universe seeking to understand itself. It's people who come first,' he says, 'that's what I have learnt.'

Sitting out on a deck at his and Paul's Hobart home—a pleasant, comfortable home not unlike its owners, seemingly unremarkable but built to look outwards—gazing at a splendid stand of white gums writhing over the Derwent beyond, I realise that we have run out of stories, and with reluctance I realise I must say something masquerading as a question, because this is, after all, an interview. So I suggest that I had always thought there was about him a melancholy that has in recent years lifted.

He reflects for a moment and then says that melancholy is the right description, and that he thought such was the natural state of an activist or indeed himself. Then he met Paul Thomas and discovered it was not so, that it was a consequence of having been alone for so long.

I ask him why he was so alone.

'Because I was gay,' he replies, and for a moment nothing more is said.

Then he speaks of how wonderful it is that

young people now can simply be whatever they are, how happy he feels when he sees men holding hands in public, how it's now rightly seen to be part of a spectrum of possibilities that one might be.

He speaks of how Bertrand Russell was a great influence on him, but how in the end Russell despaired of the cruelty of people. 'But I like people,' says Bob Brown, 'I like life.'

Though he derives a deep joy from the natural world, it is people, he says, that must be the basis of the Green movement, not the environment. He fears unless people stand up and fight for themselves and the world in which they live, we will all perish, and that is to him, it is clear, an unacceptable loss of joy and wonder. He gestures with his hands towards the white gums, the birds, the river, and says he does not want in ten thousand years for us to lose this because we will be lost with it.

'I have a will,' he says finally, 'for humanity to win.'

And it is then that I realise he has transformed once more.

It is as if having at last found love, he has discovered new, larger dimensions to his politics. I leave him in the late afternoon, conscious that he has promised to drive with Paul down to his small Huon farm to bury some dead lambs.

On the return trip he says they might stop off at the Kingston Hotel for a counter meal, and as I drive back down into Hobart I picture the two men from the country sitting in a suburban pub, one once a natty doctor, then the prophet-saint, now something far more remarkable—a man at peace, eating, drinking, laughing after his labour with his partner, in the midst of life, loving it and them each other.

I can hear them and see them, in another country that one man transformed and that then transformed him, even as I sit here writing this late of a night, and I think how a man might battle to save rivers, trees, refugees, other countries, only to discover that his whole journey was to save his own soul.

The Age
17 November 2001

Sheep Management

To DIVINE THE ORIGINS of the humiliation of a nation's moral sense as evidenced in the recent behaviour of our prime minister in Washington, rivalling past scenes of minor satraps of Soviet satellites visiting Moscow for their latest riding orders, one could do worse than read a recent instructive article by Mark Mordue on the supposed death of Australian fiction.

Reading it, I realised that the cringe is back, and without knowing it, without wishing it, we were all once more becoming its captives. Though Australian novels are now published around the world, the best of Australian novelists celebrated as globally significant—something unimaginable twenty years ago—Australia now seems ever more some strange, newly founded colony of the mind.

Mordue's piece echoed what I read and hear again and again about the failings of our writers and our publishers. Of the declining standards of editing, of the feebleness of our novelists. None of this accords with what is the truth, and yet this is becoming our understanding. All of it reinforces a declining interest in our world, in our experience, our ways of understanding life. As a culture we seem imprisoned in some nightmarish vortex. From where comes this new shame, this shocking fear of ourselves as we are now? Where is our courage when we most need it?

In a breathless rush, Mordue walks into a bookshop and discovers 'a stream of non-fiction work by Australian authors . . . that left our contemporary fiction scene six feet under'. Australian novels were 'not up to the same standard, let alone able to match the furious energy our literary non-fiction exudes'. Literary fiction is 'a plethora of second-raters and wannabes, postmodern failures and hype-riders'. 'Even the big literary books felt bogged down in their own grandness, designed to impress more than relate. Australian fiction: what a sick old scene it seemed.'

I had not thought it possible that one writer could eliminate an entire literary tradition, but Mordue achieves just that, thrilling in his own announcement that fiction is dead. Then, adducing little more than his own enthusiasm as evidence, Mordue describes the great success of Australian non-fiction.

Mordue's argument has the advantage of energy, adjectives and the only slightly more cogent reasoning of Drusilla Modjeska, whose essay on the purported failure of Australian fiction (published as 'The Present in Fiction' in her essay collection *Timepieces* of 2002) he gleefully grafts to his own feeling of inadequacy as a journalist who has written a book.

Why this inadequacy, I cannot say. After all, both Hemingway and Márquez were journalists who wrote books. His desire that journalists be granted literary respectability is understandable but misplaced. Their lack of respectability is why journalists sometimes write great books.

Mordue senses a hierarchy of letters, with novels at its apex and non-fiction written by journalists at its base. Here his instincts are at least sound: Australian letters are characterised by an appalling and destructive snobbery.

There ought, of course, to be no such hierarchy, as there ought to be no poverty, or no war. If a thing is good, as Flaubert wrote, it is good; be it a novel or a five-hundred-word article on a football match. All good writing—whatever form it appears in—deserves respect, but respect isn't a coin you gain by robbing someone else. Mordue's argument merely turns the snobbery he rightly resents upside down: fiction bad, non-fiction good.

Mordue talks of the sales success of non-fiction. But the picture here is complex. When publishers say non-fiction is booming, they more often than not mean the likes of *The Liver Cleansing Diet* or *The Guinness Book of Records*. There is little new in this. Jacqueline Kent, in her biography of the doyen of Australian editors, Beatrice Davis, notes that one of the most successful titles for Angus & Robertson during the 1950s was *Sheep Management and Diseases*.

None of the literary non-fiction books Mordue cites as great successes have sales anywhere near those of our major novels. In the last three years, when Mordue would have Australian fiction dead, we have seen the phenomenon of the two most successful literary novels in Australian history, Tim Winton's *Dirt Music* and Peter Carey's *True History of the Kelly Gang*, both selling in excess of 200,000 copies. These would be remarkable figures for literary novels in Britain, the USA or Germany, which though the largest book markets in the world, sell far fewer literary novels per capita than Australia.

Yet sales tell us nothing other than the obvious and can never be taken as the yardstick of worth. After all, two of the biggest publishing failures of the 1850s in the USA were Melville's *Moby-Dick* and Walt Whitman's *Leaves of Grass*, books that have since been recognised as some of the great works of the modern era.

Serious non-fiction speaks to contemporary issues and can have great immediate impact. But longer term it tends to fade. Could this be why Patrick White's *Voss* (1957) matters to us now in a way that Russel Ward's *The Australian Legend* (1958) no longer does? Or why *My Brother Jack* (1964) continues to reverberate long after Donald Horne's *The Lucky Country* (1964) has been relegated to the abyss of intellectual history?

It is unlikely any of the non-fiction books Mordue cites will be in print a decade from now, when Winton and Carey will continue to be read and shape our sense of ourselves. But this no more renders these non-fiction works unimportant than poor sales of a new novel now might indicate its ultimate irrelevance.

Writing is not a world composed of hostile nations but a large house full of many rooms, all or any of which writers and readers ought to and do visit. Revealingly, most of the non-fiction writers Mordue cites have also written fiction, often with great success.

But in an Australia where it is deemed an ever greater virtue to erect and guard a border than to cross back and forth between different worlds, Mordue has set himself the task of rolling out the razor wire by doing what people always do at such times: deplore the undesirable nature of what is being locked out.

Ever one for the shock of the obvious, Mordue claims contemporary non-fiction represents 'a radical hybridisation of style affecting literature internationally and sending our old generic orders into meltdown'.

Language suffers even more in this sentence than truth, for good writing was never imprisoned in 'generic orders'. From Plato to Herodotus, from Bede to Machiavelli to Gibbon, the use of poetic devices and storytelling techniques to describe or analyse reality was commonplace. What results crosses borders and escapes categories. Is Ecclesiastes theology or poetry or the greatest short story ever? Is Bernal Díaz's medieval account of the conquistadores, *The Conquest of New Spain*, firsthand reportage or, as Carlos Fuentes claimed, the first South American novel?

It is true that in any given year Australia produces few good, far less outstanding novels. In this it has much in common with the USA, Germany, France, and any other country you may wish to name. It is also readily apparent that, like other countries, we continue to publish a large amount of mediocre work. But the number of dreary first novels, weary later novels, and pompous tomes by old hacks threatening to asphyxiate rather than entertain the reader in their bed seems, relatively speaking, no worse than in previous decades.

None of this amounts to evidence of the decline of Australian fiction. What matters, all that matters, is that during this same time some good and some very good novels have also been written in Australia. To list is to exclude and having no wish to offend I won't. But I would argue that the last decade has seen more good novels than any preceding equivalent era in our history; that, far from our fiction being dead, this has been a golden age for Australian writing.

Paradoxically, though, there has been a collapse of belief in the worth of our fiction writing, and here Mordue is only echoing a number of writers before him, particularly Modjeska, who has written how once she used to read every Australian novel that came out 'but, one after another, they disappointed and irritated me'.

All this makes Mordue 'wonder if there was a growing conflict between the nature of "art" and the project of engagement in this country?'. Is there, he further muses, 'some missing connection, a breach in fiction's ability to commune with a public it had somehow forgotten or left behind?'

Having slain the Australian novel, Mordue proposes a model for its resurrection, again taking his lead from Modjeska. The vehicle?

An American novel: Jonathan Franzen's *The Corrections*.

The Corrections is not a bad book. It is a conventional realistic novel of a type some Americans have been rewriting since Sinclair Lewis's *Main Street* (1920). Overall, it is reasonably written, passably edited, and has several things to say about the USA that have been mostly said before. It is intolerable in being presented as a great book, which it is not.

Colonialisation is not just a process, it is also a state of mind, which demands one willing to be colonised as much as a coloniser. As a contemporary Australian novelist you begin to feel somehow ashamed. The deployment of more playful forms, the use of fable or allegory or historical elements, is seen to be a creative failure, a retreat. The liberating possibilities, the political edges of story are denied. You sense a collective loss of nerve, a fear of using the full arsenal of fictional techniques to confront fully our experience.

What remains are Mordue's exhortations for engagement, that tired cry of the mid-twentieth century, used by Mordue to decry all fiction not narrowly realist in the manner of Franzen. It would consign to worthlessness so much literature that we deem as essential: from Ovid to Dante, from Shakespeare to Kafka to Borges. But then, as writers through the ages have known, reality is never accurately depicted by realists.

It is not that Mordue's argument abounds in shortcomings. It is that it misses a movement of much larger significance: the loss of belief in our own stories. And Mordue's piece merely contributes to this crisis of belief rather than seeking to understand it.

It is as if we have for several years been asleep, in a torpor, no longer the lucky country but the lost country. What has happened to us? In Hungarian novelist Sandor Marai's pre-war elegy to the Austro–Hapsburg Empire (or, more precisely, Mitteleuropa), the novel *Embers*, only recently rediscovered and published to acclaim in English, we read the following:

> 'My homeland,' says the guest, 'no longer exists. My homeland was Poland, Vienna, this house, the barracks in the city, Galicia, and Chopin. What's left? Whatever mysterious substance held it all together no longer works. Everything's come apart. My homeland was a feeling, and that feeling was mortally wounded.

Why is it that people are feeling that Australia has been so wounded? Why do we feel betrayed by Australia?

For Australia is no longer an idea with which all Australians wish to identify. Australia is the Tampa, refugee internment camps in the desert, a government taking us into a war in which none of us believe. Australia is angry and confused, lost and unknown to itself, its lips collectively bound by a copper wire of shame, a country careering erratically through a world at once recognisable but no longer familiar.

We define ourselves, our culture, as failures. Instead of measuring our own work against our own experience to see whether it is wanting or worthwhile, we hold it up against the work of other places and ask only if it accords with fashion.

I have read essays imploring Australian novelists to write more about money in our novels, again, in order to be like the Americans. So much offensive idiocy and prescriptive stupidity has not been heard since the days the lecterns of Eastern Europe grew greasy with the nonsense of cultural commissars insisting on how only social realism adequately described socialist reality.

'Art is a veil,' as Wilde observed, 'rather than a mirror. She makes and unmakes many worlds, and can draw the moon from heaven with a scarlet thread.'

But in Australia it is becoming ever harder to draw the moon down with a scarlet thread of ink, to illuminate a neon night with a blinking cursor. To write novels in Australia that are not death masks of styles long since dead elsewhere has for some time been to suffer a long sneer directed at your work. I'll choose to disagree that only the prison house of contemporary American realism is an acceptable literary style. We need our stories as fabulous lies speaking to our truths, not the dull provinciality argued for by some, the sorry retailing of facts as fiction.

I could finish with a hopeful story, of how Australian publishing is a cultural success story, perhaps our greatest, that for some peculiar reason we choose not only to ignore, but to denigrate. In an era when national cultures suffered greatly from globalisation, ours grew stronger, in no small part because of our publishing industry over the last thirty years.

But telling such a story now feels a vanity, for that was a time, a short time, which one senses is already now receding, where writers and books were deemed central to the idea of Australia.

For all the success I have described, the book world is changing rapidly. First-time Australian novels, and novels by lesser-known writers, are selling less and less. In part, changes in retailing are driving this. But in part it is a loss of belief in our own stories. The sense that there are no Australian novels worth reading drives a downward spiral of less and less publicity, promotion and support. Booksellers stop ordering, publishers start cutting lists, and writers cease writing.

Yet Australia needs new stories. It is not enough to describe and report who and what we are, necessary as this is. We also need to reimagine and reinvent ourselves, knowing that reality is our invention, not our destiny. Now more than ever, we need new dreams of Australia. And for that we must recognise the ongoing centrality of novels, and we need to build a larger, more generous house of Australian writing for this to occur.

This is no nationalistic argument, for good writing, good art are ever anti-national; rising beyond them, opposing fundamentally the nonsense of national pretensions with the mess of life. But we do need to be honest—about who and what we are, about what we have achieved and what we have not. And for that we need novels, in all their playfulness and novelty.

As the drumbeats of war build to their inevitable crescendo, it is worth reflecting on what has happened in Australia over the last several years. Could it be that the arguments Mordue advances are the cultural corollary of Howard's obsequience to American policy? That we are witnessing a profound loss of belief in the value of our own world and the art we might make from it, not dissimilar to what crippled Australia a century ago?

More than ever we need to recognise the worth of our own fiction that tells us what might become of us, that offers a vision from within as well as without, a fiction that is of our hopes and our nightmares. And those novels will necessarily be as diverse as sand in their forms, in their playfulness, in their invention. Australia remains a dream that we might yet make our own, if we only have the courage and wit to imagine it so.

On the other hand, perhaps the prime minister is right and we need this war. From *Sheep Management and Diseases* to *Anthrax for Humans*, it's been a long way round for the old country, but it must warm some hearts in the Lodge, if few places else, that we are finally getting back to who we truly are, sans literature, sans identity, sans foreign policy; a nation no more but a colony of toad eaters once again, in awe of, and in servitude to a new imperium.

The Sydney Morning Herald
March 2003

Poor Fellow, My Suburb

I ARRIVE with a coach-load of media in Glen Alpine, which the photographer sitting next to me describes as the Paris end of Campbelltown. A new estate, Glen Alpine is full of large two-storey brick houses with gable porticos and columns and faux-concrete drives bedecked with Federation finials—the McMansions so derided in inner Sydney.

The bus pulls up just around the corner from Mark Latham's home—more humble than its neighbours—and fifty media decamp. Up at the Lathams' there are uniformed police and stocky plain-clothes security dressed like models for a regional menswear catalogue.

Mark Latham's backyard looks like a stage set of suburbia; coppice-logged retaining walls and in part modestly decked—homely not flash. Arranged artfully on the otherwise neat lawn are enough bats and balls to service Glen Alpine primary school, as if to make the point of blokes and boys and balls. Like a lot about Mark Latham's presentation of himself, it seems a little overdone.

Is it possible that eighteen-month-old Oliver and three-year-old Isaac use all these? It seems churlish to ask such things, so instead I listen to Mark Latham say many of the things I am going to hear him keep on saying, about policy and mortgage-belt-ville and Mark Latham understanding, to which will be added the rest of the Latham litany—trust, truth, Mark's mum and the virtues of private homeownership, masculinity, incentive, reading, his kids, and, of course, more policy.

In his backyard we have Mark's children and Mark's photogenic wife, Janine Lacey, and Mark, having finished with policy for the day, is telling us how the boys brought him brekkie and some prezzies, and now he says, pointing to a table with some trays of food, help yourself to the sambos.

A cameraman and a sound recordist pick up a football and pass it to one another, the only spontaneous act in an otherwise wholly orchestrated day, intended to demonstrate to us who have been bussed in the authentic suburban credentials of Mark.

Mark Latham divides Australia into tourists and residents. Residents are people who live near Mark. Tourists are people who read this paper and have no idea that the real (real being a word Mark likes) Australia is writ in the image of Mark's romance with himself and his own story, a romance that in many ways seems to have become close to a political pathology, limited and limiting.

It's a rerun in many ways of Howard's elites, but then much of Mark Latham is. But many of the tourists, or insiders as he might also have it, are perhaps the group most intoxicated by Latham. The more he scorns and derides them, the more many of them wish to anoint him. Witness Margaret Simons' latest *Quarterly* essay or Michael Duffy's book on Abbott and Latham in which the latter writes in a tone almost besotted with Latham. For them Latham is both authentic and young. But authentic to what?

Latham is in many ways the embodiment of those he claims to despise: the ultimate insider, with party jobs and positions since he left university; a career politician anointed and helped by Whitlam, who views him as his heir; a bookish man who is said to be a loner.

At the end of that interminable morning in

the backyard it occurs to me that nothing has happened. I mention this to a journalist sitting next to me on the bus as we head back to Sydney.

'That's right, mate,' he says, as though I have just told him that the sun comes up in the morning. 'Nothing ever does. It's played out elsewhere.'

There is, in the Mark-babble I am to hear over the next few days I travel with the media pack, the thread of a story to be drawn out, and the story is Mark, and the story goes like this: there is a romance of the suburbs and I am both its song and its singer and its saviour.

If ever this romance of the Australian suburbs had an anthem, it was West Australian Dave Warner's 1978 hit, 'Just a Suburban Boy'. Summoning all the righteous wrath of the perennially wounded outsider that was de rigueur for such young male anthems, Dave Warner raged at how it must be easier for boys from the city. He cultivated suburban dag as a new chic. It didn't work. Chubby men in Hawaiian shirts hadn't since the Beach Boys. But his marriage of a punk anger to a distinctly Australian suburban experience that was at odds with the urban aesthetics of new-wave music resonated.

In interviews for rock magazines of the time Dave expounded on his theories of the suburbs and Australian identity, arguing that the inner-city world might be fine if you are Bruce

Springsteen or an English new-wave singer, but in Australia it was meaningless. He condemned the patronising of the Australian suburban experience by the likes of Barry Humphries and argued for an art from the inside, rather than from outside looking in.

In the 1980s, Mark Latham's favourite song was 'Just a Suburban Boy'.

'It was his song,' writes biographer Michael Duffy, 'about his people and his place.'

'Of course, it's not the same anymore,' says Dave Warner when I finally track him down some days later. 'Then we all shared something, but now it's McMansions here and poverty there.'

Mark's song these days is an often awkward mix of policy wonkery and blokey wankery, and, like so much else about the man, one suspects the result of conscious choice.

It doesn't always work. Mike Carlton, on whose 2UE radio program Latham previously dropped the bombshell about bringing the troops home by Christmas, asks Latham a few days after I first see him in his backyard 'to talk in plain English, no gobbledegook'. But that's hard for Latham who seems to love policy, its language, its symmetry, its complexities and neat resolutions, its—one sometimes suspects—abstraction from real life.

In the afternoon I go back out west to Panania to visit a friend who is a carpenter. He is one of those for whom Latham invented the term later used to describe Howard's constituency: aspirational voter. We have a few beers. He asks me a question that before visiting Latham's home I would have felt more confident in answering.

'Is that Latham a phony?' he asks. 'I've worked on those McMansions. Does he think living in them ever made anybody happy?'

The media bus is a Contiki tour from hell, full of camera crews, photo journalists, print journalists, radio journalists, along with some Latham staffers. Inside it sounds like a cicada swarm at dusk with mobiles chirruping, radio journos filing by phone and photographers testing cameras.

We are notified by SMS messages as to the time of departure of the media bus, but rarely its destination or purpose. One day it's a 6 am start to head off to a health-care policy in Gosford, another it's arriving in Surfers Paradise at midnight in preparation for a tour of a pineapple cannery.

Everything that can be controlled is controlled, and Mark Latham is the on-message messenger. But the hope and the promise of Mark Latham is that he will also be the message.

A journalist on the bus tells me Australia will be different under Latham, that he will fundamentally change Australia. How? I ask. He can't say precisely, but then nobody can, least of all, on the evidence of his campaigning, Mark Latham.

The problem is that Mark isn't performing. He seems listless, flat. Day after day, Latham is underwhelming in his speech and manner. Rumours abound that his health has still not recovered. Stories are beginning to run about Mogadon Mark.

But his dullness seems another choice he makes. You sense in his answers at press conferences and in interviews that everything is calculated—his aggression, his occasional colloquialism, his passivity, his studied mundanity. Sometimes when a question is asked it is as if two answers are run by in his mind, and he chooses the one that gives nothing away. When asked about Howard's suddenly new-found concerns about David Hicks' trial, Latham merely and meekly says that the story of Hicks is one about 'bad government decisions'.

His emotion and vulnerability, his two most attractive features, are transformed by his decisions about how to campaign into a sullen brooding and an aloofness. The problem is that Latham is emotion, and without it he can seem very little.

You discover some of the truth of a man in the insults he chooses to hurl: Latham is not an arselicker and he doesn't defer or demean himself by trying to ingratiate himself, or play at false bonhomie with the journalists.

Still, many of the journalists are fascinated by him. In some ways it is not because of what he is, but because of what he isn't. The journalists are sick of Howard: some dislike him, some respect him, some are beyond political judgements, but nearly all are bored by him. Latham's not Howard and he's not Beazley and he's not Crean. He's not old and they tend to be young.

One morning, waiting for the bus to leave from the Sydney Harbour Marriott, an AAP photographer is sipping at takeaway coffee.

'Hanson was great,' he says. 'She said whatever she thought and we did whatever we wanted.' He takes another sip. 'Up there in redneck wonderland,' he adds wistfully. I glimpse the attraction of Hanson: to a media imprisoned in a numbing process she must have seemed the last expression of spontaneity in Australian politics: stupid, bigoted, angry, human.

I realise that contemporary politics has become a very dull spectator sport, and in it a figure like Latham—erratic, occasionally colourful—looms large. Perhaps it is a measure of the relentless tedium of so much of Australian politics, and the dullness of so many of its actors, that a man characterised by alternating periods of brutish language and numbing insipidity can be the source of such hope. Perhaps too it is the nature of many of the journalists. Often accused of undue cynicism, they can seem oddly naïve. They want to believe that something of what they report on might mean something good.

I begin to sense how when a bus-load of people are on the trail of one man, they invest themselves in that person until, like or dislike him, he becomes not one man but the sum of all their imaginings and longings and passions. To the extent Latham is seen to be interesting it is because bored journos more interesting than he have created him.

Sometimes Latham comes a little alive in response to a question, and the pack bristle with excitement, like dogs that have been dropping sticks at their master's feet for days in the hope he might play. He's got his mojo back, they declare optimistically after one press conference. Sometimes he can be funny, generally when he's being dismissive of the Liberals. But it's rare.

Latham seems like an instrument never quite in tune; he has an idea of himself he wishes us to share and take back to the nation, but is he the equal of the idea? There is a melody of yearning rewarded and striving vindicated, the notes are all there, but something seems out of key. And, in any case, just what is the idea? Can he be the creation he dreams ought to lead us? You know he wishes us to believe he is Mark the suburban boy, but is the real truth similar to Balzac's observation of Victor Hugo—is Mark Latham a madman who thinks he is Mark Latham?

Typical is his performance launching his tax package on Tuesday. The room is packed with over a hundred people: the seated senior journos, the row of cameras and their cameramen arrayed like mediaeval archers behind them; and behind them the milling minders, politicians and other hacks.

All the names of Australian political journalism are assembled, from the spreading figure of Laurie Oakes, sleek and assured as a Tongan king waiting to pass judgement, to Glenn Milne, an inquisitive pygmy possum intent on minor mischief. Many of the men of the gallery are suited; they look like the people they describe, indistinguishable in both attire and their assumptions.

It's a key moment for Latham, his biggest setpiece announcement on a day when the polling has got worse. Latham looks waxen, listless and unwell. His manner is edgy and abrasive, and if it is not aggressive nor is it endearing. The conference goes badly. Latham struggles to express anything simply.

Under questioning it becomes apparent that the package details do not seem to bear the grandiose ambition of Latham's claims. At such times his nervous tics become more pronounced: his tongue darting out blue-tongue-like to lick his lips; the slight raising of the head and closing of his eyes as he says no; along with the habit that has become standard with many Australian politicians of repeating a pointless phrase—A POINTLESS PHRASE—with pointed emphasis.

Latham grows dismissive, talking about how it is in the real Australia and the real world, as though all those in front of him have never had to pay a bill or worry about money, and live in some happy otherworld, unlike the real world about which Mark and only Mark knows so much and no one else knows anything. This isn't an abstract sociology tutorial, he says at one point, but it is beginning to sound like it is, and Mark our tutor on all that is real—kitchen tables, public housing estates, bills, fortnightly trauma—and all that isn't, which is John Howard's $600 family payment.

But in spite of his performance, Latham's tax package carries the papers the following morning when we visit the Golden Circle pineapple cannery canteen in Brisbane. Like a hive of maddened insects compelled by strange lunar movements to swarm, there suddenly appears the media scrum of booms and cameras and lights and stills cameras held aloft like holy relics. And at its centre Latham. A single, strange beast, the scrum moves toward the centre of the canteen.

Then something unexpected happens: from a table at the far left a Filipino woman called Percy begins clapping and cheering, and her claps and cheering are taken up by her table of four. In the remote heart of the scrum, Latham hears them and turns. His face lights up. He starts walking toward them.

They cheer and clap and giggle more, and the other tables of Filipino and Vietnamese women around them begin clapping and cheering too, until the canteen is joined in uproar. Latham sits down at Percy's table and then moves to the other tables, talking, smiling, clearly lifted, the heaviness of the previous days gone.

After Latham has moved on, I go and talk with the women who began the cheering. Elvie, Percy, Divina and Carmelita are from the Philippines and voted for John Howard last election. Why? I ask. Because Kim Beazley was too soft, they say. This time they say they will vote for Mark Latham. They like his tax policy.

'And change,' says Percy, who began the clapping. 'I think maybe now change is good.'

Later Latham seems energised. Perhaps he needs people, needs their love or their hate. And perhaps he does care. Latham looks like a Labor politician of another era, and it does seem that if he will just allow himself to behave more like one, to break with the sterility of modern campaigning and reach out to people more, a different man might emerge. Yet now he is carrying something far worse than his own ambition, and that is the burden of hope of so many, and who can say how best to bear the load?

The irony is that Percy and her tablemates are not Latham's people, not the happy, hardworking westies of Glen Alpine, with their median income, where your postcode is your destiny—his middle Australia writ in the image of his own romance.

They earn too little, most being seasonal workers picking up $10,000 for their time in the cannery, and you won't hear much out of Latham's Labor on the vexed issues of race and migration.

Still, at that moment I wonder if Mark Latham succeeds in taking government, it may just be that the point he wins is when in a Queensland pineapple cannery a Filipino migrant woman begins cheering for change.

But as I fly home that evening, the television news flickering above on the plane's monitors is filled not with images of Percy cheering in Brisbane, but of terrorist horror in Beslan. The plane has gone into a holding pattern. And like everyone else within it, I feel suddenly fearful.

The Age
11 September 2004

The Rohypnol Rape Decade

'IT'S LIKE THIS,' said one journo as we sat around the Brisbane Sheraton hotel foyer midday Monday, after being SMSed that the prime minister would not now be doing any afternoon engagements.

'A short man lies in Brisbane, and we report that, and a beefy man lies in Perth, and we report that, and that's journalism. Everyone knows there's more, but how do you reach it?'

No one could say. The journos told stories to each other that were true but which they would never write. Instead they wrote what they had to. The best did what they could, the worst had given up and just filed a gloss of the release for the day.

There was a sense something had gone wrong and we were all part of it.

There was nothing left to do for the rest of the day. The journos took to gossiping on mobiles and the *Sunday* program took to filming the journos gossiping on mobiles, and when the TV crew had enough footage of that, they went upstairs to the hotel pool and filmed their journo sitting at the hotel pool toasting with a cocktail the top storeys of the hotel where Howard and his party were encamped, thanking Mr Howard for such a gruelling schedule.

None of it went unnoticed. Howard's staffers, ever friendly and efficient, helping you get the story they wanted, were soon on to it. Later in the afternoon, Tony O'Leary, Howard's chief media advisor, was asking the show's reporter why he had been filmed drinking by the pool.

In the end all that remained was Howard and our short, occasional encounters with him, the gallery journos invariably horseshoed in the press conferences around him like the rising keyboards of a great wurlitzer organ that was his alone to play. And play us he did, magnificently.

There was no doubt he was dull, sometimes spectacularly so, but he had transformed his dullness into a political virtue. He evaded questions that led to issues he didn't wish to discuss with an agility and a speed that surprised; once, when he was asked about Iraq, I opened my notebook, got my pen to the paper, only to realise he had already made some answer I had not heard and was now into a new question on the happier ground of his childcare rebate scheme.

He shrugged off insults and taunts, and had an ability almost uncanny on the days I saw him to calmly shut down debates he didn't wish to engage in, and return journalists to his campaigning messages. It was as if so much of the preceding eight-and-a-half years had somehow gone missing in action and, try as some did, they were never going to be found again.

'Prime Minister,' a journalist asked at a press conference at the Brisbane Sheraton on Tuesday, 'Tony Blair has told a meeting of the Labour Party in Britain that politicians aren't always able to tell the truth. Do you agree with this statement?'

In a sublime moment the great organist pulled his head up and replied authoritatively:

'I always tell the truth.'

And as he said it he slowly scanned the journalists around him, as if daring someone to take issue with him. No one did. For a moment there was a hint of something at the edges of his mouth—was it a smirk, a smile?—but Howard is too disciplined to allow himself any public displays of smugness, and within a question he had the conference on to Medicare and from there, in half a sentence, to interest rates.

Watching him, I was reminded of the Peruvian novelist Mario Vargas Llosa, who in 1990 ran for the presidency of his country on a Thatcherite platform and always felt the need to say something different and new each time he spoke. His campaign was a disaster.

His English campaign manager, Mark Malloch Brown, later wrote of how 'political communication is two things: definition and repetition. Mrs Thatcher never tired of saying the same thing . . . this aspect of Mrs Thatcher above all others required emulating. It was the one that least interested Vargas Llosa.'

It is, however, the aspect in which Howard may even outdo one of his great models. That morning I had joined John Howard and a small harlequinade largely composed of porky middle-aged men sweating heavily—journos, minders, bodyguards, TV crews—on his famed morning walk. John Howard sets a pace that can fairly be described as cracking.

I put it to Howard that if Mark Latham gets asked about his child's schooling he wants a journalist censured, but that I had the impression that if he, Howard, got hit over the back of the head with an iron bar he would simply crawl back up and say that under him interest rates will stay lower.

'Bingo!' said Howard, raising a finger in cricket umpire fashion, laughing and adding,

'And there will be no deficit.' It was a joke, and it's a joke being played out daily across the nation as a way of ensuring the Liberal Party is returned to power.

It's hard to see Howard separate from the caricatures, the lampoons, the impersonations, the ridicule, the commentaries, the praise as the man of iron, the hate as the suckhole who sold the nation out.

But all these ideas—particularly the hate—are the least helpful ways to try to understand the riddle of John Howard: a man seemingly so ordinary and unremarkable in the flesh, whose record in government has been one of the most extraordinary and controversial in the history of the Commonwealth.

Even those close to Howard describe him in unexpected ways. Senator Robert Hill, speaking after John Howard at a Liberal Party luncheon at the Adelaide Hilton, told his audience what a good investment they had made in John Howard. It was a curious description, as if Howard were not a man but an '80s junk bond that had unexpectedly transformed into a profitable blue chip.

I asked a senior gallery journalist what Howard was like, and they replied:

'What you see is what you get.'

But what is it that they were seeing?

All I could see was a mundanity so honed it was like staring at polished concrete.

In person Howard is pleasant and inoffensive, and he works at not creating reasons to dislike him. Once a byword for bad dressing, Howard is now a dapper little man, immaculately turned out. If there seemed a slight brittleness—manifest in a limb occasionally jerking slightly like a *Thunderbird* puppet, and a constant rolling onto the balls of his feet, back and forth, up and down, as if ever restless to get back to the real business—this too seemed unremarkable. When walking he carries a slight limp in one leg, as if carrying some hip injury. Typically, he acknowledges none of it.

As the most well-known politician in the country he has about him a lack of charisma so complete that it is almost baffling and can at times appear to amount to a near anonymity. In an era when Kylie's arse means more than Kylie's voice, John Howard is an odd triumph of substance over style. His oratory is dismal, his interviews tend to be soporific, his presence unremarkable.

Yet how little any of this matters. Because when he makes a point it is for a point. Everything he does is, you feel, calculated for an exact political effect. And in the new world of controlled grabs and staged events, he is a master of the times.

Contemporary campaigning in its sterility and its control is heaven-sent for a man so singularly lacking in charisma, but so focused and skilful on getting electorally significant messages out to voters via the media while revealing nothing.

It is then of no consequence that in the Brisbane City Hall I dozed off during Howard's interminably long campaign launch speech—a state in which I felt myself envied by many around me—to wake to the discovery that six billion dollars had been spent in the space of a catnap. Because boring it may have been, short on rhetoric as it certainly was, but in its spending he revealed himself as a man of power brutally calculating what it costs to retain that power.

A speech, or for that matter any public occasion, seems for Howard not about the egotistic assertion of self, but about getting out certain messages— in this case to those whose votes he wishes to buy—and carefully avoiding mentioning the far-reaching consequences of what his proposals often entail.

Unlike Latham, who has a large rhetoric but not always the measures to match the language, Howard talks small even when what is being proposed is large. Much with John Howard tends to sound and seem insignificant, but it rarely is. His success is somehow bound up in his seemingly innocuous personality masking large ambitions.

Later, Howard, who like Latham always travels separately from the media in Commonwealth limousines, decided to jump on the media bus on the return from a visit to a Brisbane removalist company's offices.

It's reported as a spontaneous act of informality. Perhaps it was meant as that. Or perhaps it was in response to a front-page article in the *Australian* denouncing the excessive control of the media by Howard's staff on the previous day. Whatever the motivation, it turns into one more set-piece press conference with more interesting images than those on offer from the removalists, and it gets good mileage the following day.

On the bus, at the surreal heart of a rolling, swaying jellyfish of journos and boom tentacles, a smiling Howard told us he felt happy with his campaign launch speech because it caught something of his philosophy.

Howard and his supporters often talk about his philosophy, and how his actions are always consistent with it. When asked what that philosophy is, you are invariably given a handful of meek words such as choice and family, or the more abstract but hardly threatening individualism, and sometimes, more daringly, compassion and a fair go.

A scattering of words doesn't equal a philosophy. It doesn't explain what has happened to Australia since 1996. Beneath little things, big things sometimes hide. These words seem inadequate, say, as an explanation of children held behind razor wire, or of exactly why we are in Iraq.

But perhaps they serve to obscure what John Howard is about: power. How he is about power's practice, about its obsessive desire, and how he looks sleek and assured with its invigorating tonic. Power seems to infuse him with energy, allows him to leave puffing journalists and sweating cameramen in his wake every morning, a daily humiliation of the media that one suspects is not without its small pleasure, and power animates his every utterance and action.

With Howard, unlike most modern politicians, the medium—the man—is not the message. The man has simply become the honed expression of political ambition.

And so Howard absents the story of his own personality from the podium and the studio. Everything he says and does is for a political point, not to romance himself. Like an artist about whom the only interesting thing is their work, into which they have poured their very essence, perhaps there is not that much else to John Howard other than what he has done as a politician.

Unlike many politicians, Howard gives no evidence of wishing to be loved, and not seeking it, it doesn't manifest itself around him. His place and his success are grounded in something different: at the friendly functions and events staged for him, the faithful like him. Yet, like its object, their support and admiration is neither effusive nor demonstrative. As one Liberal supporter put it to me: 'You don't cheer your funds manager because he makes money for you.'

Elsewhere people seem to neither like nor despise him. If there is an emotion it is indifference, and one senses that suits John Howard, allowing him to get on with the business of power.

On my last night on the trail of John Howard, the media and Howard's party were encamped at the Adelaide Hilton. The Hilton bar filled with nattily attired young men and evening-dressed women from a South Australian restaurant and hotel chain who were having a big night out. As the waiters and waitresses and chefs and barmaids and barmen smoked and loudly chatted each other up, a small entourage bustled down the side of the mob.

A few journalists noticed that it was John Howard, but no one else. No one jeered and no one waved. It was Australia, it was 2004, and the man no one seems to know was returning to his hotel suite unnoticed to continue working as he for so long had; patiently, carefully, precisely ensuring that he would win an historic fourth term.

I had Howard wrong; I have always had him wrong. Like many—though by no means all—Australians, I always dismissed him as marooned in the past, a captive of outdated prejudices. But he had been to Australia what rohypnol is to a waiting drink.

In the bar the children of Howard's Australia played and drank and flirted, and it was hard not to think that, win or lose, Howard had somehow won. It was true that these prosperous, docile and fearful times had been his, but it was harder to credit how much he had shaped a time and a people to his own smallness. But shape us he had. Latham, touted as Whitlam's anointed, was really Howard's spiritual heir who would, should he win, do much to continue Howard's idea of Australia into the future, and he would do it to Labor applause. How Howard had done all this was even more of an enigma than the man himself. There was about him a genius of mundanity.

By the end, I was glad to leave the campaign. In truth I felt I had spent too long on the media bus now, sensing the inadequacy of what I was doing, and the impressive capacity of Howard to give nothing of himself away, the futility of trying to discover anything in a place and time that is completely about the pursuit of power.

Waiting for a taxi to the airport, I had a beer in the bar with a few other journos. Out there beyond us something was happening, but if you wanted to know what it was, the last people in Australia to ask would be the coach-load of journalists and hangers-on such as myself. We asked many different questions, but the truth was we always got the same answers, and in the end we heard them so often we had started believing them ourselves.

So many of the journalists, left or right or apolitical, appeared imprisoned in wisdoms that seem to be received from Howard: that elections are about the economy. That no one wishes to hear about Aborigines. That the right if difficult thing was done about refugees. Most of the journalists thought the hatred of Howard just silly. They see him as an ordinary man who had luck and over the years learnt a formidable tenacity and great wile. And this too is Howard's long-term achievement, this confusion with his own personal smallness and the immense changes he has brought to Australia.

When I got home there was a fundraising letter asking for help to keep an eighteen-year-old student refugee called Ruth Cruz in Tasmania. Ruth Cruz arrived in Australia four years ago, having fled criminal gang violence in her home of El Salvador, and now lives in Hobart with her sister, Daysi. Denied a refugee visa by Howard's government, a large public campaign succeeded only in eliciting from the government a visa to finish high school. Now her only option to stay is to become a full-fee-paying international student, hence the fundraising campaign.

There was much in Ruth Cruz's story that seemed to accord with Howard's loose ideas of choice and family and individualism, that invited the compassion and a fair go he so often talks about. But if $50,000 cannot be raised by next March, the federal government will deport Ruth Cruz.

The letter was a dash of reality in contrast to Howard's grey and ultimately fictitious sense of the world. Like the nation since 1996, I felt I had sleepwalked through my time with Howard. I believed none of it, yet after a few days with Howard I understood something of his soporific power. Like some dull, inert force, he simply overwhelmed you until you retreated to anything other than engaging with what he was saying and doing.

Only now, it was time to wake up.

The Age
2 October 2004

Van Diemen's Land

At a moment when Australians seem once more prepared to voyage forward, there has arrived a book for these new times. In one of those moments of coincidence that a novelist is rarely allowed but life frequently offers, we have, in the same week in which history is being made with the apology to the Stolen Generations, a remarkable history being published that offers a new and mature understanding of our origins.

For after what was falsely termed 'the history wars', but which was rather a perverted attempt to politicise the past in order to justify the renascent bigotries of what already seems a strange, lost decade, we have, in James Boyce's *Van Diemen's Land*, a landmark of historical scholarship that suggests a largeness and openness in our origins as a nation of which we need not be scared, nor ashamed, far less divided by bitterness and hate.

Though Boyce's story is frequently terrible, this is not a work of accusation, but a history of hope. It suggests that we are not dispossessed Europeans, but a muddy wash of peoples who were made anew in the merge of an old pre-industrial, pre-modern European culture with an extraordinary natural world and a remarkable black culture.

As much as a process of colonisation, Boyce's work suggests a history of indigenisation— a strange, uneven, frequently repressed, often violent process in which a white underclass took on much of the black ways of living. It suggests we have a connection with our land not solely based on ideas of commerce, and that there are continuities in our understanding of our land that extend back into pre-history. It is an argument, never more timely, that we are our own people, not a poor imitation of elsewhere.

Boyce's *Van Diemen's Land* is for a time a land where many, according to a contemporary witness, 'dress in kangaroo skins without linen and wear sandals made of seal skins. They smell like foxes'. They live in 'bark huts like the natives, not cultivating anything, but living entirely on kangaroos, emus, and small porcupines'. No less an authority than John West, founding editor of *The Sydney*

Morning Herald, wrote in 1856 that the whites living outside of the settlement 'had a way of life somewhat resembling that of the Aborigines'.

Boyce details at length how this Van Diemonian peasantry along with black Tasmania was defeated—but not destroyed—by the colonial authorities. If the individual testimony of the bounty hunters and adventurers who bring the nascent Van Diemonian world to heel sometimes begins to feel like a *Heart of Darkness* journey into madness, it never descends into the grotesque or the Gothic, clichés behind the bars of which the rich, human truth of Tasmania—at once terrible, beautiful and extraordinary—has been kept gaoled for too long.

For Boyce is a historian of the intimate, and through the detail of gardens, clothing and diet he makes us question so many assumptions we take for granted about that time, about our relationship with the land, and with each other. Be it the suppression of fiddling and dancing in Hobart pubs in the 1840s or the popularity of the Tasmanian Aborigines' most prized decoration, red ochre, amongst whites in Launceston in the 1830s, Boyce constantly makes us see the past fresh and anew. We are given not an invasion nor a happy history of noble pioneers, but a messy, inescapably human response to extraordinary times and places, out of which emerged a new people. It is brutal, confused, and a place of shifting alliances and understandings; a landscape of revolutions in which occurs a transformation of sense and sensibilities so extraordinary that it will be some centuries before we will be able to fully compass its liberating dimensions.

This is no accident. Tasmania was invented in 1856, the new name an attempt to erase the already well-known history of Aboriginal war, convict hell and homosexuality. The old name of Van Diemen's Land was to be erased, and along with it an idea of not only what was worst about us as human beings but also the possibility of what might be better; the manifold rebellion, not just political, but social and cultural, that had ensued in coming to understand how to live in this strange new world.

This is not a romanticising, but it does go beyond the idea of apportioning blame, which has poisoned historical discussion in Australia for too long. In Boyce's *Van Diemen's Land*, the white with most sympathy for the black may well be the man who murders a black in another place, while the man with best intentions, such as Governor Arthur, may be the one guilty of the worst crimes. An Aborigine such as Black Mary may be a black bushranger and police informant, the lover of an outlaw as well as his fatal betrayer. It is above all else a relentlessly human account that takes into its thinking the way in which good and evil lurk in every human breast.

For Boyce the past is not a prize of politics like the Lodge, to be fought for and won. For the truth is not relative. It is absolute, and though our interpretations are infinite, we must try to understand, as much as it is possible, that truth on its own terms.

And his exploration of what was described, not by a 1960s academic, but an 1830s attorney general, as 'a war of extermination' of the Tasmanian Aborigines is gripping in its terrible, human unfolding: the way it was avoidable, the way it became inevitable, the tragedy of a land where the English, as ship's captain's wife Rosalie O'Hare confided in her diary in 1828, 'consider the massacre of these people an honour'.

Boyce's compelling account of the bushranger Michael Howe, whose authority equalled that of the early Van Diemen's Land governors, is a potent reminder of how much the vaunted Australian traditions of revolt had Tasmanian origins. For good reason did the Victorian government legislate to prevent Van Diemonians emigrating during the 1850s. Ned Kelly's father was a Van Diemonian convict, and the Jerilderie Letter has sections that strongly echo the writings of Frank the Poet, the Van Diemonian convict bard whose odes to liberty were the first writings to be banned in Australia.

So much that is so rich is contained here that it will be misrepresented by both its supporters and detractors. But how good it feels to read a history that is not politics, but an act of enquiry applying intellect, empathy and a fresh curiosity to trying to discover all that from which we are torn. We have possibilities in Australia with our unique land, with our indigenous people, with our own particular response to our world, that suggest our future might still be worth dreaming.

This is a history that will be challenged, rebutted and shown to be wrong in various places. All works of largeness and innovation invite such a fate. But its generosity of spirit exploring the possibilities of what we once were suggests all that we might yet be. It is the most significant colonial history since *The Fatal Shore*. If it is not as rollicking a read as Hughes' masterpiece, it is perhaps more original. In re-imagining one aspect of Australia's past, it invents for us all a new future.

The Sydney Morning Herald
16 February 2008

Lest We Forget

LEST WE FORGET, we reverentially intone every Anzac Day and yet we forget all the time. We forget that out of the 102,000 Australians who have died in wars since Federation, only 40,000 died during World War II.

We forget that all those other wars in which the majority died were not because we were threatened, but because we were involved with empires elsewhere threatening others. We forget that all those Australians who died often died bravely or honourably, or wretchedly or terribly, but they did not die for our country but for other countries.

We forget we asked the Americans to be in Vietnam and we don't even know exactly why we are in Afghanistan.

We say we remember the fallen, and if we do that at best sporadically and inadequately, we hardly give thought to the many, many more who did not fall, but who returned home maimed, sometimes not only in body but also in mind and soul.

We forget the great truth of the ages: that war, even if it is sometimes necessary, is always evil. And we forget that the essence of its evil is that it inevitably demands of some soldiers that they do terrible things that would horrify and repulse them in any other situation.

We forget that Australians—like all other nations—have committed atrocities in numerous wars, from World War I onwards. This doesn't mean Australian soldiers are any more or less dishonourable than soldiers of any other nations. It simply reflects the realities of war and what war does to us all as human beings.

We forget that the horror of an atrocity is not just that visited on its victims, but also on the people who commit those atrocities. Not necessarily bad people or psychopathic people, but ordinary human beings who must live with the horror of their actions for the rest of their lives.

And we forget these ordinary human beings are young men who have friends and families, that the horror within them comes to affect many and passes like a shot through the decades and sometimes generations.

And because we forget all these things all the time, we sent young Australians off to Afghanistan without debating any of this. No politician should ask any soldier to go to war, with all that means for those young men, without the very, very best of reasons.

Historically, though, our politicians' reasons have in such matters rarely been the very best. Mostly they have been self-serving actions dressed up as national interest. We forget that young men's lives are useful to them in helping secure influence and stature in international forums.

We forget too that the prosecution of distant wars has always made weak leaders look strong domestically. For what defence minister, sleek as a well-fed goose, doesn't look a little more of a man overseeing war games? What prime minister doesn't feel a little more of a real leader talking troops and missions and materiel?

But beyond the high moral tone and ersatz grandeur, our politicians have been careless. They need to answer to the dead—our dead and the dead we killed. They need to answer to the living—those soldiers who return, whose future lives are blighted and the lives of whose families and friends will be scarred irrevocably, decades after the 24-hour news cycle, the three-year parliamentary term, the two-term government, the near decade-long war.

Between January and June this year, according to a recent United Nations report, 1271 civilians died of violence in Afghanistan, with the Taliban responsible for 76 per cent of the deaths. We—the West and the government we support in Kabul—are responsible for the other 305 deaths.

Three Australian soldiers presently face manslaughter charges over the death of six civilians, five of whom were children, in a night raid. Whatever legal judgement results, those men carry the burden of five children's deaths with them for the rest of their lives. No politician should ask that any Australian carry such weights without the most compelling justification.

And yet they do.

Lest we forget, they dutifully murmur, along with staying the course and seeing the mission through. And in thinking we are honouring the dead we forget again and again that politicians who speak softly have always been careless with the lives of others.

The Drum
19 October 2010

The Lost Larrikin

MY FATHER WAS one of Dunlop's Thousand, that now mythical group of POWs who endured the horrors of the Death Railway under the Japanese, led by a doctor called Weary Dunlop.

Recently he told me how one day on the railway a digger called Slappy Oldham turned up to sick parade with a cigarette dangling from the corner of his mouth. An English major called Driscoll made a swipe at Slappy, which the POW evaded by the slightest move of his head.

'Lucky you missed,' said Slappy Oldham.

Driscoll angrily demanded to know why.

'If you'd touched me,' said Slappy Oldham, 'I'd have dropped you, you bastard.'

Driscoll grew more agitated and was speaking of charges when Dunlop arrived. Slappy walked up to the colonel.

'You know that bastard, Driscoll,' said Slappy Oldham. 'He tried to swipe me, and I told him off.'

'Good on you, Slappy,' replied Weary, to the amazement of the upper echelon. 'Always look after yourself.'

I once spent a memorable evening with Dunlop that ended drinking in his Toorak mansion, a place where time seemed to have stopped somewhere in the 1930s. I sat on an aged, cracked leather couch and he told me of how as a young doctor in London in the 1930s he had gone into the East End and taken on Oswald Mosley's British Union of Fascists blackshirts at their rallies. I knew this was unusual, for Dunlop was a distinguished rugby player, capped for Australia, and Mosley recruited heavily from London rugby circles. So concerned was Dunlop by the rise of Fascism he told me he very nearly went to Spain to fight with the International Brigade.

Was he attracted to the Communist Party then? I asked, knowing well how many of the very best had at the time been.

'Not at all,' Dunlop said. 'I just didn't agree.'

After a dirty, lost decade Australia finds itself standing bewildered and slightly befuddled by the age in which it has suddenly woken up. After the most sustained boom in Australian history Australians may fairly ask: Where did the money go? It will be an interesting question to ponder when our cherished property values begin to drop and portfolios start to plummet and we stare out at our great UV-irradiated land and wonder why our public schools are worse, our hospitals worse, our social security worse, and our cities less liveable.

How is it we have come to face perhaps the greatest environmental catastrophe since creatures even slower-witted than ourselves ruled the planet, and still, for example, happily not just endorse but subsidise with our taxes the destruction of Tasmanian native forests?

Perhaps we have agreed with too much that was wrong for too long.

If we look at Australia over the last several years we are presented with the unedifying, indeed disturbing image of a society whose major institutions failed. This was not necessarily so in other countries. If it is the case, for example, that the present US administration has committed crimes—at Abu Ghraib, at Guantanamo, in rendition centres—then it was US journalists who first brought them to public light, it was US legal systems and US lawyers that began bringing them into question, it was US public figures who began pressing for change. Nothing similar happened in Australia.

If we look to another example, that of Britain, we see that they had what we didn't: a major debate in parliament about whether they should go to war in Iraq. On the tombstone of the former British foreign affairs minister, Robin Cook, who resigned his parliamentary positions over the Iraq invasion, are his own poignant words: 'I may not have succeeded in halting the war, but I did secure the right of parliament to decide on war.' One after another, loyal Tory MP and loyal Labour MP stood up and said they disagreed with their party leadership's support of the war.

To the shame of all Australian parliamentarians, not one here could claim the same epitaph as Cook, for in contrast our parliament was quiescent. In Australia such a questioning of the party leadership's position on any issue has become not just unacceptable, but pilloried in the impoverished political judgement of the Canberra press gallery as political suicide. To speak out is to be declared a rat, a party renegade and a political naïve.

Yet not so long ago both parties were accepting of difference and criticism from within their own ranks. When he was prime minister, Malcolm Fraser is said on occasion to have told lobbyists that he agreed with their position, but as his senators would not back him he could not help.

Now there are only two sins in Australian political life: being different and being charged. Thus a Labor member can be expelled from the ALP for having a cappuccino with former Western

Australian premier Brian Burke, but happily photographed with current Tasmanian premier Paul Lennon, whose colonial mansion was renovated by forestry giant Gunns at, he has said, a cost of 'well over $100,000', but which the *Australian* newspaper later quoted an unnamed source as saying was worth $400,000.

And so our parties failed us. Our parliament failed us. Our media failed us. The question as to why is difficult to answer, though it clearly is to be found in an uneasy examination of a new conformity at the heart of Australian life. There is a new censorship that involves not overt government repression, but a gradual and real capitulation by so many individuals—journalists, middle managers in the media, public figures—to the idea that many things in Australia are now better left unsaid.

What we have witnessed is a very real corrosion of the idea of the truth and respect for those whose views differ from that of power. What we have experienced is a coarsening of public rhetoric by standover men who claim to speak for the ordinary Australian, but seem to represent the interest of government and corporate power. They are given opinion columns and radio talkback programs. They are accorded the status of minor celebrities and there sometimes seems no end to the uniquely Australian cross of their public belligerence in defence of private interest at popular expense.

While many, for example, righteously demanded David Hicks apologise to the nation on his release, none seemed to think it worth demanding the same of Alan Jones when, in the wake of the Cronulla riots, he was found by the Australian Communications and Media Authority (ACMA) to have broadcast comments 'likely to encourage violence or brutality and to vilify people of Lebanese and Middle-Eastern backgrounds on the basis of ethnicity'.

What we hear parroted at ever more shrill frequencies are the old mantras of Stalinism, once used to justify the great crimes of a century, being ironically recycled by the right to defend the indefensible. Those who speak out are inevitably demonised as out-of-touch elites. This pejorative use of the word elite begins with Stalin in 1948 when he used it to describe Jewish intellectuals upon whom he was about to turn his terror.

We are being told, as the old USSR was told, that there are things that matter more than the truth and individual freedom—national security, the needs of the security forces, special international commercial undertakings. But there is nothing higher in this life than the truth and individual freedom. The striving for these two things is the essence of who and what we are.

We now have provision for secret trials and secret imprisonment in this country. With the Dr Haneef case we have been presented the disturbing spectre of an innocent man appearing to be framed and imprisoned for what can only be seen as political advantage, in which our security forces would seem to have lied to the Australian public. Late last year a Sydney court found that an Australian citizen, Izhar Ul-Haque, had been illegally kidnapped and threatened by ASIO operatives. This blatant abuse of power by our secret police, and what it might bode for our future, seemed of little concern to either major party or the media, and the lack of attention the case received was all the more remarkable given it happened in the middle of the federal election.

We are no longer in the twentieth century of class and ideology, of endless economic growth, of left and right, of centre and periphery. It is a confusing new world of religious zealotry and economic uncertainty perhaps unseen since the 1930s; of competing superpowers; of politics as little more than corporate cheerleading, with various gods renascent and the sudden recognition that the earth is not only finite in its fecundity, but also in its charity towards its ultimate parasitic species.

Internationally it is not that we are no longer capable of pursuing an independent foreign policy, it is rather that our new obsequiousness to power, masquerading as the realpolitik of contemporary international affairs, means that we cannot even dream of the possibility. We are caught between a rising superpower, China, and a declining super-power, the USA, with not so much a policy as an ingrained servility on the part of our political class that does not bode well.

Historically the world seems to be setting upon an era of unprecedented global barbarity. This would seem an extravagant claim, particularly in the wake of the twentieth century, which was after all the most murderous in history. Yet beneath the ceaseless blathering about democracy from the White House and from our own leaders, our political systems are increasingly unresponsive to the democratic impulses in their own societies. If our economy is globalised, so too is our human destiny. We have in absolute terms far more people living in poverty than at any time in human history. Our own society is ever more stratified, and the divisions of wealth and power grow daily, and daily grow more offensive, and represent a slow accumulation of grievances that will, if not addressed, invite a terrible denouement.

At the same time we have been taught to accept that endless change in our economic lives is in-evitable and unavoidable, but that political change of any consequence is impossible. Cynicism is the new naïvety. We believe in abstract forces too much, in human capacity too little. We have lost faith in the only real power in this world: our faith in ourselves.

For as a society and as a polity we need to once more rediscover and reassert the necessity of witnessing and questioning as the greatest guarantee we can have of democracy. If I am left believing in anything, it is something very simple: that truth matters above all else. Anything that honours and guarantees the truth is not just good, but necessary. For the road to tyranny is never opened with a sudden coup d'etat. It is a long path paved with the small cobbles of silence, lies and deceit that ends, inevitably, in horror. In Australia we stand at the head of that road. Only history will tell us if as a people we chose the terrible folly of continuing to walk down it.

But nothing is ever given, and hope is ever as real a possibility as despair. People have once more begun finding courage and giving voice to what concerns them. Whether it's The Chaser—our very own Radio Free Europe—or journalists once more beginning to question and show courage, as they did with the Dr Haneef case, there is a new mood in our nation that we ought to welcome.

I don't mean by this the recent change of our national government. We in Australia make too much of our political leaders and their work, and too little of our own failings and triumphs. The world advances to a better place through the countless acts of everyday goodness shown by millions of people too easily dismissed as everyday.

In the end none of these things is ever a matter of party. Dunlop most likely voted Liberal, yet it is no paradox that Tom Uren, once known as the heart of the Left, said he learnt his socialism from Weary Dunlop while a POW. Uren, like Dunlop, didn't agree. And while a Labor man through and through, Uren has described the Greens' Bob Brown, another man who doesn't agree, as having the blood of Mandela flowing in his veins.

These are matters of character, and to use a word little heard these days, courage. More than ever, in this new age, Australians need to once more recover their voice, and that power of not agreeing with power. It's time, like Slappy Oldham, we looked after ourselves a little more, and deferred to power and its Driscolls a little less.

The Bulletin
Final issue, February 2008

Gunns: the Tragedy of Tasmania

THIS STORY BEGINS with a Tasmanian man fern (*Dicksonia antarctica*) for sale in a London nursery. Along with the healthy price tag, some £160, is a note: 'This tree fern has been salvage harvested in accordance with a management plan approved by the Governments of Tasmania and the Commonwealth of Australia.' If you were to believe both governments, that plan ensures that Tasmania has a sustainable logging industry, which, according to Australian forest minister Eric Abetz, is 'the best managed in the world'.

The truth is otherwise. The man fern—possibly several centuries old—comes from native forests destroyed by a logging industry that was recently found to be illegal by the federal Australian court. It comes from either primeval rainforest that has been evolving for millennia, or wet eucalypt forest, some of which contains the mighty *Eucalyptus regnans*. These aptly named kings of trees are the tallest hardwood trees and flowering plants on Earth, some more than twenty metres in girth and ninety metres in height. These forests are being destroyed in Tasmania in spite of widespread community opposition and increasing international concern.

Clearfelling, as the name suggests, first involves the complete felling of a forest, by chainsaws and skidders. Then the whole is torched, the firing started by helicopters dropping incendiary devices made of jellied petroleum—commonly known as napalm. The resultant fire is of such ferocity it produces atomic bomb-like mushroom clouds visible from considerable distances. In consequence, every autumn, the island's otherwise most beautiful season, china-blue skies are frequently nicotine-scummed, an inescapable reminder that clearfelling means the total destruction of ancient and unique forests. At its worst, the smoke from these burn-offs has led to the closure of schools, highways and tourist destinations.

In the Styx Valley in the south-west, the world's last great unprotected stands of old-growth *Eucalyptus regnans* are being reduced to piles of smouldering ash. Over 85 per cent of old-growth *regnans* forests are gone, and it is estimated that less than 13,000 hectares of these extraordinary trees remain in their old-growth form. Almost half of them are to be clearfelled. Most will end up as paper in Japan.

In logging coupes around Tasmania, exotic rainforest trees such as myrtle, sassafras, leatherwood and celery-top pine—extraordinary, exquisite trees, many centuries old, some of which are found nowhere else—are often just left on the ground and burnt.

The hellish landscape that results from clearfelling—akin to a Great War battlefield—is generally turned into large monocultural plantations of either radiata pine or *Eucalyptus nitens*, sustained by such a heavy program of fertilisers and pesticides that water sources for some local communities have been contaminated by Atrazine, a controversial herbicide linked with cancer and banned in much of Europe. Blue-dyed carrots soaked in 1080 poison are laid on private plantations to kill native grazing animals that pose a threat to tree seedlings. The slaughter that results sees not only possums, wallabies and kangaroos die in slow agony, but other species—including wombats, bettongs and potaroos—killed in large numbers in spite of being officially protected species.

In 2003, an ageing Tasmanian forester, Bill Manning, was subpoenaed to testify in front of an Australian Senate committee investigating the Tasmanian forestry industry. He methodically began to unravel a tale of environmental catastrophe, of industry connivance and government complicity. His detailed evidence suggested that the Tasmanian forestry industry was not only systematically destroying unique forests, but poisoning the very fabric of Tasmanian politics and life.

No greenie hardliner, Manning was rather a man who worked for thirty years in the Tasmanian forests, who believes the forests ought to be logged, but logged so that they remain for the future. Yet he alleged to the Senate committee that forestry management had been corrupted. At the hearing, he painted a picture of the illegal destruction of public forests on a scale so vast that it was transforming the landscape of Tasmania. Branding what was happening in Tasmania 'an ecological disaster', Manning talked of how an 'accelerated and unaccountable logging industry' was destroying wholesale native forests, 'which are unique in the world for their flora and fauna'.

'The clearfelling is out of control,' he told the senators. 'The scale of clearfelling in Tasmania is huge.'

A whispering campaign about Bill Manning's

state of mind began, and in the four years since he ended a career he loved by standing up for what he believed, nothing has changed except for the worse. Today, Tasmania is the only Australian state that clearfells its rainforests. While the rest of Australia has either ended, or is ending, the logging of old-growth forests, Tasmania is the only state where it is secretly planned to accelerate the destruction of native forests, driven by the greed for profit that can be made from woodchips.

As with any epidemic of madness, there sometimes seems no end to its horror. Among Tasmania's many unique plants and animals is the endangered giant freshwater crayfish, one of the largest invertebrates in the world. Although technically protected, its very future is threatened by the frenzy of logging surrounding the creeks where it lives. When a government-appointed expert panel recommended buffer zones of forest be preserved to protect the crayfish, these zones were reduced to a bare minimum, and the areas continue to be logged. 'Clearfelling is going on at an incredible rate in their habitat,' crayfish expert Todd Walsh says. 'It's going berserk.'

Tasmania is an extraordinary land, one that many hoped might become, in the words of the legendary landscape photographer Olegas Truchanas, 'a shining beacon in an otherwise dull, uniform and largely artificial world'. Its remoteness, its wildness, its unique natural world—all seemed to offer the possibility of a prosperous and good future to an island that had for a century been the poorest in the Australian Commonwealth. Instead, over the past three decades, Tasmania has mortgaged its future to the woodchipping industry, which is today dominated by one company: Gunns Ltd. And it is Gunns—not the Tasmanian people— that has been the beneficiary of the destruction of Tasmania's unique forests.

Though founded in Tasmania in 1875, it was not until 1989, when it became part of the written history of corruption in Tasmania, that many Australians first came to hear of Gunns, then still one of several Tasmanian timber companies.

In that year, then Gunns chairman Eddie Rouse became concerned that the election of a Labor–Green Tasmanian government with a one-seat majority might affect his logging profits. Rouse attempted to bribe a Labor member, Jim Cox, to cross the floor, thereby bringing down the government and clearing the way for pro-logging former premier Robin Gray and the Liberal Party to resume power. Cox went to the police and the plot was exposed; a royal commission and Rouse's fall from grace and imprisonment ensued. But Gunns continued. Today it is a corporation worth more than a billion dollars, the largest company in Tasmania, with an effective monopoly of the island's hardwood logging, and a darling of the Australian stockmarket.

Yet Gunns remains haunted by the Rouse scandal. The Gunns board continues to this day to have among its directors former associates of the late Eddie Rouse. The 1991 royal commission found that director David McQuestin, whose friendship with Rouse it characterised as 'obsequious', was not 'unlawfully involved as a principal offender' with the bribery attempt, although his 'compliance with Rouse's direction in the matter was "highly improper"'—a 'glaring breach of the requisite standards of commercial morality'. Robin Gray is also now a director of Gunns: the royal commission found that he 'knew of and was involved with Rouse in Rouse's attempt to bribe Cox', and that while his conduct was not unlawful, it was 'improper, and grossly so'. John Gay, Gunns' managing director in 1989, and now its chairman and CEO, was cleared by the royal commission of any involvement with the bribery attempt.

In a dissembling world ever more given to corporate deference to a green image, the company shows an often-unexpected candour. Gunns makes no secret of its enmity towards conservationists and conservation groups. Gunns plans to destroy more, rather than less, Tasmanian native forest. Gunns makes no apologies for what this means.

'How do you feel about protected species dying for your business?' John Gay was once asked on national television.

'Well, there's too many of them,' he replied, 'and we need to keep them at a reasonable level.'

And while—like so much else in Tasmania—total woodchip production figures since 2000 are officially secret, Gunns' own evidence in support of its proposed pulp mill reveals that it plans to double woodchipping from its present annual levels of approximately 3.5 million tonnes to 7 million tonnes over the next decade.

To evade the ever-growing public anger, the woodchipping industry has had to exercise an ever-stronger control over Tasmanian life. Both major parties in Tasmania, and much of the Tasmanian media, frequently give the appearance of existing only as clients of the woodchippers. The state's interest and that of this industry are now so thoroughly identified as one and the same that anyone questioning the woodchipping industry's actions is attacked by leading government figures as a traitor to Tasmania. And it is not only the forests that have been destroyed by this industry. Its poison has seeped into every aspect of Tasmanian life: jobs are threatened, careers destroyed, people driven to leave. And in recent years, its influence has extended further, so that now its activities are endorsed nationally by both the prime minister, John Howard, and the opposition leader, Kevin Rudd.

Huge money is being made by Gunns out of destroying native forests, but to maintain what to many is an obscenity there has evolved a culture of secrecy, shared interest and intimidation that seems to firmly bind the powerful in Tasmania.

When actress Rebecca Gibney, who moved to Tasmania two years ago to raise her family, said in a television interview that she would leave the state if Gunns' proposed pulp mill was built, former Liberal Party candidate and bottle-shop owner Sam McQuestin made headlines by publicly attacking her as a 'serial complainer' whose family made no contribution to the Tasmanian economy and who had no 'right to tell the rest of us how to live our lives'. McQuestin's family is well known for its contribution: his father is David McQuestin, a Gunns director. The attack on Rebecca Gibney was but a public example of something far more widespread and insidious.

I witnessed a senior ALP politician make it clear that yet another Tasmanian was no longer welcome in the clearfell state after local businessman Gerard Castles wrote an article in a newspaper questioning government policy on old-growth logging. 'The fucking little cunt is finished,' the politician said in front of me and my twelve-year-old daughter. 'He will never work here again.'

In Tasmania, to question, to comment adversely, is to invite the possibility of ostracism and unemployment, and the state is full of those who pay a high price for their opinion on the forests, the blackballed multiplying with the blackened stumps. It is commonplace to meet people too frightened to speak publicly of their concerns about forestry practices because of the adverse consequences they perceive this might have for their careers and businesses. In consequence of the forest battle, a subtle (and sometimes not so subtle) fear has entered Tasmanian public life; it stifles dissent, avoids truth.

And how can it be otherwise? The great majority of Tasmanians appear to be overwhelmingly opposed to old-growth logging, and only by the constant crushing of opposing points of view, and the attempted silencing and smearing of those who put them, can the practice continue. And so, nearly two decades after its then chairman's failed attempt to corrupt parliament, Gunns now seems so powerful that Tasmanians joke that their government is the '*gunnerment*', and leading national politicians of all persuasions acknowledge that the real power in Tasmania is not the government but Gunns itself.

This goes further than the sizeable donations Gunns makes to both major parties, both in Tasmania and nationally. It goes beyond Gunns' role in election campaigns, such as the $486,000 spent on aggressive political advertising in the 2004 federal election by the Forest Industries Association of Tasmania (FIAT), of which Gunns is the largest member.

'A lot of people are intimidated by the employment side of the [Tasmanian forestry] industry,' prominent Liberal Senator Bill Heffernan has said, 'including some politicians.'

But who can blame even the powerful being scared? The former Tasmanian Liberal leader Bob Cheek recalls how 'the state's misguided forestry policy was ruthlessly policed by Gunns'; how fearful the politicians were of the forest lobby and what he describes as their 'hitmen'.

In a cowed society, the Tasmanian government often gives the impression of being little more than a toadying standover man for its corporate godfather, willing to undertake any action, no matter how degrading, to help those with the real power.

When, in 2004, Wyena farming couple Howard and Michelle Carpenter had themselves and their property directly sprayed by a helicopter with

Atrazine meant for an adjacent Gunns plantation, poisoning their water supply, Gunns' only response was to send the couple two bottles of spring water. Later, when the story became a public scandal, they provided the Carpenters with a water tank, which a few months later they removed, though the Carpenters' water bore remained poisoned. To reassure the public that they had no cause for concern, then water minister Steve Kons fronted a media conference at which he loyally drank a glass of water tainted with Atrazine. Steve Kons is now deputy premier.

According to former federal Labor leader Mark Latham, 'They [Gunns] run the state Labor Government, they run [Labor Premier] Lennon, and old Lennon there, he wouldn't scratch himself unless the guy who heads up Gunns told him to.'

Latham would know: after all, his own bid to be prime minister came to its end when he ran up against Gunns in the federal election of 2004. Latham was no conservationist, but the growing national outcry over Tasmania's forests, driven by a long campaign by conservation groups, led him in the final week of the election to propose a bold plan to end logging the island's old-growth forests, which included an $800-million compensation package to logging workers. Quite extraordinarily, the package was rejected by the Tasmanian Labor movement.

Two days later, Liberal Prime Minister John Howard flew into Tasmania to announce the continuation of old-growth logging indefinitely, along with more extensive subsidies to the logging industry and, as a sop to the green vote, the protection of some areas of old growth. A few areas were victories. Much was a con: areas that were either already reserved or, as Terry Edwards of FIAT admitted about the north Styx, very difficult to log; or, as in the Weld or Florentine, later—in an act of arch cynicism—to be logged anyway.

In the most extraordinary images of that election, Howard was cheered by two thousand logging workers at a rally in Launceston, supported by the powerful Construction, Forest, Mining and Energy Union (CFMEU). Within the week Howard's Liberal Party would be returned to government, and within a year some of those same workers would be forced out of the industry by Gunns breaking contracts, and looking for work in a workplace ravaged by the toughest anti-union laws in Australia's history—introduced by the man they had cheered on to victory.

'We seem to get on better with the Liberals than we do with Labor at the moment,' Premier Paul Lennon told a journalist a few weeks after federal Labor had suffered one of its worst defeats.

The conservationists had foundered and, with Howard's crushing victory, Gunns now had a federal government who felt electorally rewarded for taking the company's side. Gunns had too a state government so committed to it that seemingly no issue in Tasmania could be decided without first being held up to see whether it was good or bad for the old-growth logging industry. And it left federal Labor so terrified of ever touching the issue again that when Kevin Rudd assumed leadership of the federal Labor Party in 2006, one of his first actions was to endorse the Tasmanian logging industry. But then, as former Labor leader Mark Latham ruefully admitted, 'No policy issue or set of relationships better demonstrates the ethical decline and political corruption of the Australian Labor movement than Tasmanian forestry.'

The dogs were off the leash and Gunns was now at its most powerful. Within months it made a move that was widely viewed as an attempt to cripple the conservation movement, the last remaining impediment to its ambitions. On 14 December 2004, Gunns filed a 216-page, $6.3-million claim against a group of conservationists and organisations who became known as the Gunns 20.

The writ was an extraordinary document that sought to sue a penniless grandmother who had opposed logging in her district; a national political leader, Senator Bob Brown; a doctor who had raised public-health issues about woodchip piles; prominent conservationists; Australia's leading wilderness-conservation organisation, the Wilderness Society; a film-maker; and several day protesters.

All were joined in what was alleged to be a conspiracy guilty of the crime of 'corporate vilification'. The writ presented a tale of a group of people together seeking—through a series of actions as diverse as protesters chaining themselves to logging machinery to the lobbying of Japanese paper companies—to destroy Gunns' profits. The perversity of the action was staggering: with the immense fortune they had made out of destroying Tasmania's forests, Gunns had launched an action that would, if successful, have redefined the practice of democracy as the crime of conspiracy. An Australian would not have been able to criticise, question or campaign against a corporation for risk of being bankrupted in legal proceedings brought against them by the richest and most powerful in their society, claiming damage to their corporate interest. No matter how a corporation made its money, be it from tobacco or asbestos or chemicals, all of its actions would have effectively been removed from the realm of public life. Gunns' action was compared with the legal standover tactics that prevail in such countries as Singapore, where political opponents are bankrupted then jailed through such a process of litigation.

If its legal ramifications were enormous but unrealised, its political impact was immediate. While the writ excited a national outcry, garnering comparisons with the McLibel case, in the short term it only further intimidated many in Tasmania, and tied up the leading conservation groups and conservationists in a difficult, expensive and all-consuming court case at a moment when Gunns was planning its most controversial action of all.

Two days after it issued the writ, Gunns announced its plans for a gigantic $1.4-billion pulp mill, the biggest infrastructure project in Tasmania's history and one of the biggest pulp mills in the world, to be built 36 kilometres from Launceston, Tasmania's second-largest city.

At first, reassuring commitments were given that the mill would be environmentally friendly— chlorine-free and primarily using plantation timber. Premier Paul Lennon was adamant that the pulp mill would only go ahead if Gunns could prove to an independent government body, the Resource and Planning Development Commission (RPDC), that their proposal adhered to world's best environmental standards. The process was to be above politics and the RPDC's decision final.

But public concern began to grow as it became clear Gunns was planning something entirely different from what they had originally announced. Gunns now wanted to build a Kraft chlorine bleaching mill—the type that produce dioxins, some of the most toxic substances known to man—fuelled initially by 80 per cent native forest woodchips.

Then was revealed the shocking news that to feed the pulp mill's gargantuan appetite, Gunns had signed a deal (the exact details of which remain secret) with then Tasmanian forest minister Bryan Green, which would *double* the level of ongoing destruction of Tasmania's native forests for the next twenty years.

At the same time, Tasmanians discovered that while the mill was being assessed Premier Lennon was using a wholly owned subsidiary of Gunns, the construction company Hinman, Wright & Manser, to renovate his historic home. It was a curious choice of builder. Hinman, Wright & Manser is known to be less than enthusiastic in its support of unionised labour, and to be a keen proponent of the Howard government's new workplace-relations laws, of which Lennon had publicly been such a vociferous critic. More remarkably, the Gunns 'construction division', as it is termed on Gunns' website, is an industrial- and civil-works company that advertises itself as specialising in 'larger construction work' such as mines, warehouses, concrete plants, schools, courts, remand centres, nursing homes, hospitals, reservoirs, substations, wharf berths, woodchip mills and road bridges, but makes no mention of home renovation.

Lennon has never answered questions put at the time as to what Hinman, Wright & Manser originally quoted for the job, nor whether there were other quotes. Lennon and Gunns have both subsequently said Lennon paid for the renovations, though the precise sum has never been revealed. Lennon dismissed any questions on the matter as a painful attack on his family's privacy.

The revelations that have since ensued have not been so easily dismissed. In early January 2007, the head of the RPDC pulp-mill inquiry, Julian Green, and the inquiry's leading scientific advisor and a national pulp-mill expert, Dr Warwick Raverty, both resigned, both citing political interference.

It has become public knowledge that the RPDC found Gunns' own evidence to be riddled with inaccuracies and errors; that levels of dioxins in the mill's outflow were initially under-estimated by a factor of forty-five; and that the mill, as well as failing to address Australian Medical Association (AMA) concerns about ultra-fine particle pollution, also significantly failed to meet at least three official air-pollution guidelines. Senior scientists questioned Gunns' claims that 64,000 tonnes of treated effluent pouring daily from the mill into the ocean would not harm Bass Strait and its marine life. Gunns' modelling for air pollution in the Tamar Valley was so shoddy that it sometimes fantastically predicted air pollution would be lower with a pulp mill than without.

Pointing out that 'no other pulp mill in the world uses the process Gunns proposes', and that its noxious emissions would pour into a densely populated valley already subject to the worst smog problems in Tasmania, Raverty has since warned that 'the risk of producing unacceptable levels of deadly and persistent chemicals known as organochlorines is too high'.

Raverty—who works for a subsidiary of the CSIRO and has consistently pointed out he is speaking in a personal capacity about the mill's pollution risk—has claimed a Gunns executive rang the CSIRO seeking to pressure them into silencing him. The CSIRO has confirmed Gunns has 'expressed concerns'. Raverty has since said he would welcome the opportunity to appear before a criminal-justice commission or royal commission into the process, because there needed to be public scrutiny of the 'very unethical activities' of the Tasmanian government.

Though the Tasmanian chapter of the AMA warned Tasmania's political leaders they would be personally accountable for any health problems resulting from the proposed pulp mill, the leaders were listening not to such dire concerns but rather to the Gunns board, with whom Premier Lennon and his kitchen cabinet met on 25 February 2007.

Two days later, Gunns told the Australian Stock Exchange it was 'confident the necessary government approvals' for its pulp mill 'will be obtained within a timeframe which maintains the commercial value of the project'. That same day Paul Lennon handed the newly appointed head of the RPDC's pulp-mill assessment panel, former Supreme Court judge Christopher Wright, QC, a typed timeline laying out his demands.

'It was plain as the nose on my face,' Wright later said, 'that he was trying to please Gunns.'

Describing it as a 'completely inappropriate . . . attempt to pressure' him, Wright rejected what he termed an 'ultimatum' by Lennon to dump public hearings and wind up the assessment by 31 July or face the RPDC being dumped in favour of legislation fast-tracking the process. A fortnight later Gunns withdrew from the RPDC process, blaming delays which John Gay termed 'commercially unacceptable'. What was commercially acceptable to Gunns now became a political imperative for the Tasmanian government.

That Wright said most of the delays were Gunns' fault was of no consequence. For in a manner that at least is understandable—if onerous—to Tasmanians, it is clear that in Tasmania Gunns more or less *is* the law. The woodchippers and their government cronies constantly use the courts against conservationists, but when the courts are used against them, the government's response is admirably straightforward: change the law.

They changed the law, for example, when Greens leader Bob Brown sold everything he had and took both the Tasmanian and federal governments to court to prove that under their own laws the logging industry in Tasmania was illegal because it threatened the survival of endangered species—including the Tasmanian wedge-tailed eagle and the swift parrot. Brown won, but the government's response was not to enforce the Tasmanian Regional Forest Agreement to protect those species, but simply to alter it so logging is once again legal.

Faced with the possibility the mill might now not meet the RPDC pollution guidelines, Premier Paul Lennon simply rushed an act through parliament to establish an entirely new process that seems certain to ensure the mill will be approved by the end of this August. Though this contradicted what Lennon had so dogmatically maintained for the previous two years about an impartial process that was above politics, the act—drafted with the input of a Gunns lawyer—tellingly allows for the mill to no longer meet the original pollution guidelines. Public consultation has been dispensed with and, most remarkably—and possibly without precedent in the annals of Westminster legislation—the act explicitly provides that the mill will still go ahead even if it is proven that the consultant assessing the project has been bribed.

It had been uncharacteristic of Lennon to even pretend a process mattered more than an outcome, and it seemed cynicism more of a piece with his predecessor, the late Jim Bacon. A one-time Maoist, an upper-middle-class alumni of one of Australia's most exclusive private schools, Melbourne's Scotch College, and later of one of its most infamous unions, the Victorian Builders' Labourers' Federation (BLF), Bacon was for several years a loyal lieutenant of the BLF's leader, the notorious Norm Gallagher. By the time Gallagher was gaoled for taking bribes from developers, and the BLF the subject of a Royal Commission that led to its deregistration, Bacon was ensconced in Tasmania, where the old BLF tactics of espousing a working-class rhetoric while cosying up to the powerful served him well. In 1997 he became leader of the Tasmanian Labor Party.

The following year Bacon was instrumental in brokering the deal that saw the very electoral basis of the Tasmanian parliament altered. Since the 1970s, when the world's first Green party was formed in Tasmania, the Greens had been a powerful political minority in Tasmania, securing up to a seventh of parliamentary seats under the island's unique proportional representation system and with it, on occasion, the balance of power.

The 1998 deal was sold to the public as a commonsense measure to reduce the number of parliamentary members. But it was intensely political in effect, because fewer parliamentarians meant a higher quota was needed by an individual to be elected, thus making it harder for minority parties to win seats and possibly destroying future Green representation—and with it the only real opposition to the woodchipping industry. The former Liberal leader Bob Cheek recalls how Robin Gray, the state's premier in the 1980s and now Gunns board member, lobbied him the night before the vote on the reform.

'We've got to stop the Greens, Bob,' Gray told Cheek. And they did.

The subsequent election in August 1998 saw the Greens decimated and Jim Bacon's Labor

Party triumphant. The Bacon government quickly established itself as the most pro-big-business government Tasmania had ever had. Favoured companies received extraordinary treatment. The privately owned Federal Hotels group, who ran the island's two casinos, was awarded a fifteen-year gaming monopoly—conservatively estimated by Citigroup to be worth $130 million in licensing revenues—free of charge.

But the greatest winner was Gunns. Gunns' shares were languishing at $1.40 when the Bacon government came to power. Its subsequent growth was dizzying. Within four years, it had recorded an increase of 199 per cent in profits. With the acquisition of two rival companies, Gunns took control of more than 85 per cent of logging in Tasmania. Five years after Bacon won government, Gunns was worth more than $1 billion, with shares trading in excess of $12. It had become both the largest logging company in Australia and the largest hardwood woodchip exporter in the world, its product flooding in from the state's fallen forests.

The Tasmanian government, which a century ago paid people to shoot the Tasmanian tiger, now provided every incentive to destroy old-growth forest. One of Bacon's first acts was making 85,000 hectares of previously 'deferred forest' available for logging. Gunns paid only paltry royalties to Forestry Tasmania, the public body charged with getting a commercial return from the crown forests that were the very basis of Gunns' record profits.

When in 2003 Gunns posted an after-tax profit of $74 million, Forestry Tasmania made a hardly impressive $20 million. By 2005, when Gunns' after-tax profit had soared to $101.3 million, Forestry Tasmania's profit had slumped to $13.5 million. Its projected profit for 2006–07 is break even—a return of zero dollars, nothing, to the Tasmanian taxpayers on the estimated $700-million value of its publicly owned forest estate.

But it wasn't just that public forestry resources were being systematically handed over to a single company's shareholders—it was that much of Gunns' profits were coming out of taxpayers' pockets. On private land, Gunns made a second profit from the federal tax breaks that made tree plantations—with which clearfelled native forests were replaced—one of corporate Australia's favourite forms of tax minimisation from the late 1990s.

On top of all this, Bacon's government accelerated a familiar pattern of ongoing handouts to an industry that constantly shed jobs, devastated the environment and sought to manipulate the political system. Between 1988 and the present day, the Tasmanian forest industry has received a staggering total of $780 million in taxpayer handouts, $289 million of it since 2005, much of which has been used to facilitate further old-growth logging. If an accounting were possible of the taxpayer-subsidised plantation schemes and added to this sum, the real subsidy paid by the Australian taxpayer to an industry that destroys Australia's heritage would approach a billion dollars.

But then, not the least shocking thing about the destruction of Tasmania's old-growth forests is that the Tasmanian logging industry is in the end not a commercially viable industry at all, but a massive parasite on the public purse, an industry as driven by ideological bailouts and hidden subsidies as a Soviet-era pig-iron foundry.

Worse still, at the moment Tasmania was acquiring a global reputation as an island of exceptional beauty, the forces that would destroy much of the island's unique natural world had been unleashed. This sad irony, denied in Tasmania, did not however escape the more astute of the world's media: major features began appearing in the *Observer, Le Figaro, Süddeutsch Zeitung* and the *New York Times*—mounting evidence that what was happening in Tasmania was increasingly being seen as an environmental catastrophe of global significance.

What might be read about Tasmania's forests in New York or Paris, though, was not information easily found in Hobart or Launceston. Apart from a few brave journalists, a generally craven Tasmanian media rarely questioned or challenged the woodchipping industry during these years. The *Launceston Examiner* ran a four-page feature on Gunns' pulp-mill proposal directly lifted from Gunns' advertising. Necessary fictions were repeated until they became accepted as truth—that, for example, the industry's main concern is sawlogs, when even Forestry Tasmania had admitted that sawlogs are chipped, and had been since 1972. The government's own annual reports reveal that approximately 90 per cent of Tasmania's logged native forest is woodchipped.

To this day, the forestry industry and the Tasmanian government withhold key information, fudge definitions of forest types and felling practices, and distort statistics to prevent the truth of old-growth logging becoming publicly known, diverting debate into the dullness of disputed definitions and clashing numbers. It's a tactic of semantic confusion that's worked well for the tobacco and oil industries. Beyond, forests unique in the world continue to disappear.

Jim Bacon's nickname was 'the emperor', but the man perceived to be the power behind the throne was his deputy, Paul Lennon. Ill-tempered, badly

behaved and brutally effective, his political capacity—like so many strong-arm leaders—was too
often and too easily dismissed.

Lennon made no more apologies for his thuggish
behaviour (he once shoved a conservationist up
against a wall in the middle of a meeting, an
encounter he claims not to remember) than he did
his enthusiasm for the old-growth logging industry,
or his close friendship with logging baron John
Gay. Anyone taking a first-hand look at Tasmania
would, he once said, 'see a lot of fucking trees'.

When Bacon retired as premier in early 2004
because of terminal cancer, Lennon became
premier, and any pretence that Gunns might be
reined in within Tasmania came to an end.

These days, Gunns is everywhere in Tasmania:
there are Gunns shops, Gunns television advertising, Gunns-sponsored weather bulletins. If
you go to watch an AFL game at Tasmania's
premier stadium, York Park, you pass through
the main entrance, officially and aptly named
the 'Jim Bacon Gates' built by—who else?—a
wholly owned subsidiary of Gunns, and come to
the Gunns Stand, the largest and most opulently
fitted stand at the stadium, much of it paid for,
equally aptly, by the Tasmanian government.

With the river of money that had poured
in from Tasmania's destroyed forests and
Australian taxpayers, Gunns had diversified

into businesses in New Zealand and mainland Australia. It set about becoming the main player in the Tasmanian wine industry, with itself the dominant producer. That the wood-chippers' wines—Tamar Ridge, Coombend, Devil's Corner—were not stocked by some shops, bars and restaurants in Hobart because of consumer antipathy was of no concern, for the venture's financial underpinning was the same as its forestry plantations: tax-minimisation schemes in which grape-growing schemes qualified for a 100 per cent tax write off. Yet again, it was Australian taxes at work for Gunns.

Gunns now made no secret of what the cost would be for those who questioned the sanctity of old-growth logging, no matter who they were. During the 2004 federal election, plantation softwood processor Auspine—a $200-million forestry company based in South Australia that runs two pine sawmills employing 313 people in the northern Tasmanian town of Scottsdale—incurred John Gay's wrath by having the temerity to put forward a $450-million plan in which old-growth logging would be ended immediately, but Tasmania's forest industry would be expanded by 900 new jobs. John Gay made it clear that Auspine had been very foolish, saying: 'Their comments have been extremely damaging to themselves and their future in Tasmania.' Two months later

Gunns' hardware stores stopped stocking Auspine timber.

Auspine's pine comes from land owned by Forestry Tasmania, but a half-share in their trees was sold by Jim Bacon in 1999 for $40 million to American global investment firm GMO. In early 2007 it was announced that Auspine had lost its pine supply in a deal that saw the timber go to a new company, FEA, which doesn't even have a sawmill. In this manner more than 300 people are to lose their jobs. Though it is half-owner of the resource, both the state-owned Forestry Tasmania and the Tasmanian government refused to intervene in the negotiations to help Auspine or its workers.

When Paul Lennon finally went to Scottsdale four weeks after the initial announcement, sawmill workers turned their backs on the man who had always boasted he stood for the jobs of forestry-industry workers. Increasingly, it appeared to many Tasmanians that the only jobs Lennon really cared about were his own and those of the Gunns directors.

Perhaps, predictably, one of the last defences seized on in this battle by politicians on six-figure salaries is that they stand solidly with the working class. But Lennon's routine claim that 10,000 jobs are at stake if old-growth logging is ended is without substance, and avoids the truth: jobs have been disappearing in old-growth logging for many years not because of conservationists, but because of mechanisation.

While woodchipping destroyed the older labour-intensive sawmill timber industry, the Hampshire woodchip mill in north Tasmania— the biggest in the southern hemisphere—employs just twelve people. A report in the *Australian Financial Review* in 2004 revealed the Tasmanian industry in its entirety had shed more than 1200 jobs since 1997.

Like Lennon's previously expansive claims— that, for example, ending old-growth logging in Western Australia had left more than 4000 people unemployed, something categorically refuted by the West Australian government—there is no evidence for the figure of 10,000 jobs. It is more than seven times the number of 1345 jobs given by the forest industry's very own report on employment in the old-growth logging sector, commissioned by FIAT and written by pro-logging academics in 2004. Old-growth logging—as distinct from the rest of the much larger forestry industry—was estimated by a Timber Workers for Forests report in the same year to employ only 580 people.

Both figures were arrived at before Gunns sent many contractors to the wall in 2006. When it slashed logging contracts by up to 40 per cent in order to offset a decline in woodchip sales, logging workers for the first time publicly expressed their growing bitterness towards Gunns and the hefty profits it made while their livelihoods vanished.

In response, Barry Chipman of Timber Communities Australia (TCA) denied there was growing resentment within the industry towards Gunns. Presenting itself as the grassroots organisation of those it terms the 'forest folk', the TCA has from its inception in 1987 been rather the vehicle of the National Association of Forest Industries (NAFI), which is financed by the logging industry. The TCA's support for the Tasmanian logging industry was once described by John Gay as an 'invaluable alliance'. Invaluable though it may be, the logging industry does put a price on it: in 2002–03, $723,154 of the TCA's total revenues of $836,977 came from direct industry contributions. In the same year, Barry Chipman's wages were directly paid for by NAFI.

It was 'situations like this', Barry Chipman said of Gunns' slashing of contracts, that sorted out the 'good operators' from the bad—further incensing those contractors who, acting on Gunns' promises of more work, had taken out bigger loans to purchase better equipment, and now were unable to meet repayments. 'Everyone needs to tighten their belt a little bit,' went on Barry Chipman. 'Any downturn will also be suffered by the company and its shareholders.'

But they didn't seem to be suffering much that year at 'Launceston's Lavish Lunch', the annual fundraiser of the Launceston branch of the Australian Cancer Research Foundation, held at one of Tasmania's most celebrated historic homes, Entally House. It seems to have been a splendid day for the island's clearfelling contessas, and the Launceston Cancerians—whose committee includes the wives of both John Gay and David McQuestin—later waxed effusively on their website about the event, extending 'A big thanks . . . to Mr John Gay for opening his house for the function'.

Entally House isn't really John Gay's house, of course, just as crown forest isn't really his land. Like the forest, the historic house belonged to the Tasmanian people, but in 2004 the Tasmanian government terminated the National Trust's lease and gave a twenty-year lease to Gunns. Plans by Gunns to plant a ten-hectare vineyard in Entally's historic grounds were immediately announced, John Gay declaring that Gunns was developing 'a detailed marketing strategy' for the property, centring on the marketing of Gunns wines. And in this way a unique piece of Australia's heritage became both John Gay's house and a charming marketing platform for Gunns. The public can still visit Entally House, which technically-speaking they still own. It only costs $8 per adult.

Meanwhile, log-truck driver Gary Coad, who in 2004 was found guilty of assaulting a conservationist and who cheered John Howard when he announced his ongoing support for old-growth logging, was forced out of the industry he had worked in for thirty years. Now, he told a local newspaper, contractors were at 'rock bottom', unable to make ends meet. 'The biggest problem in the industry,' he went on to say, 'is Gunns' virtual monopoly', which meant any contractors who criticised the company could be squeezed out of the business. 'We came up [to the Launceston rally] and fought for John Gay's livelihood,' continued Coad, 'well now it's time for him to turn around and do the same for us.'

But no one—no Gunns director, no Labor or Liberal politician, no CFMEU rep, no 'forest community' advocates—was going to fight for the forest workers or speak to the betrayal they felt as they now went under and jobs disappeared.

Instead, like Kevin Rudd on his 'listening' tour in December 2006, they said they supported the existing Tasmanian forestry industry in order, as Rudd put it, that there be 'no overall loss of jobs', ignoring the fact that supporting Gunns was exactly what ensured workers continue to lose jobs, continue to be exploited under Gunns' pitiless tendering system, and continue to suffer.

There is in all this a constant thread: the Lennon government's and Gunns' real mates are not workers, but millionaires. Behind the smoke-screen of statistics, beyond the down-home cant of 'timber folk' peddled by the woodchippers' propagandists, past the endless lies, is a simple, wretched truth: great areas of Australia's remnant wild lands are being reduced to a landscape of battlefields, in order to make a handful of very rich people even richer.

Yet giving away such an extraordinary public resource as Tasmania's forests now threatens Tasmania's broader economic prospects. A growing weight of financial analysis suggests that the economics of plantations (with which native forests are being replaced) are not assured but rather are a huge gamble for Tasmania. The industry's future prospects depend on global pulp prices rising; the government, as the *Australian Financial Review* put it, has 'tied the state's economic future to the success of Gunns and its tree farms'.

If the future looks dubious, the present is already a failure. The reality is that logging old-growth brings little wealth and few jobs to struggling, impoverished rural communities. While Gunns makes its profits primarily in Tasmania, the great majority of Gunns' shares are owned by mainland institutions. It has been estimated that less than

15 per cent of Gunns' profits remain in the island, where the largest individual shareholder is John Gay himself.

As a consequence of the forestry debate, Tasmania is an ever more oppressive place to live. Just six days after conservationists had gone public about arson threats in 2004, the historian Bruce Poulson, a prominent opponent of plans to log the historically significant site of Recherché Bay, had the study behind his Dover house, containing decades of research, burnt down in what police described as a 'malicious' attack. Ray and Leanne Green had displayed Wilderness Society posters calling for an end to old-growth clearfelling in the Styx Valley in their Something Wild Wildlife Sanctuary, half an hour's drive from the valley. They received numerous informal threats, and then had their business burnt out. Cameraman Brian Dimmick was bashed by a log-truck driver who objected to Dimmick filming his vehicle. So it goes in the clearfell state.

It has never been suggested, nor do I wish to imply, that Gunns is any way responsible for such acts. But the workings of power are not always reducible to orders or even intentions. When a society becomes entrapped in a growing coarsening of public rhetoric, evil finds succour. When

vilification is commonplace, when lies are the
currency of the day and followers seek to rise
through the vigorous anticipation of leaders'
unspoken desires, where all are disenfranchised
and the most powerless feel what little security
they have will be destroyed by those who merely
disagree, acts of dubious morality and even of
violent criminality become justifiable and appear
honourable.

Despite a few years of economic upturn between
2001 and 2006, Tasmania is once more technically
in recession, and it remains the poorest Australian
state, with the highest levels of unemployment,
and around 40 per cent of its population dependent on government welfare. New key industries,
such as tourism and fine foods and wines, trade as
much on the island's pristine image as they do on
the products they sell. There is growing concern
in all these industries—in which job growth is
concentrated—at the relentless damage being
done to Tasmania's name by images of smouldering forest coupes.

It is little wonder that many Tasmanians now
worry that the woodchippers' greed destroys
not only their natural heritage, but distorts their
parliament, deforms their polity, and poisons their
society. And perhaps it is for that reason that the
battle for forests in Tasmania is ever more about
free speech and democracy—about a people's

right to exercise some control over their destiny, about their desire to have a better, freer society— as it is about wild lands.

Of late, Gunns' fortunes have suffered. Its share price has dropped by over a quarter from its record highs of 2005, a reflection of having lost 20 per cent of its market share to South American plantations. At the same time, woodchip prices have dropped and a global woodchip glut beckons, all of which leaves Tasmania ever more dependent on uneconomic woodchip production.

A recent rally in support of its pulp mill attracted just fifty people, including Premier Paul Lennon. Gunns' own research shows only one in four Tasmanians support the island's biggest company. Meanwhile, its pulp-mill proposal meets with growing fury throughout Tasmania. The once timorous Tasmanian media has begun showing courage in questioning Gunns' activities; the Gunns 20 writ has been rejected three times and Gunns' projected legal costs—including damages it must now pay—run into millions. On throwing it out a second time, Judge Bongiorno described the lengthy writ as legally 'embarrassing'. Still, Gunns persists with a fourth suit. Eminent QC Julian Burnside, one of the defence counsels, has said, 'It leaves you wondering if the purpose is simply to terrorise.'

Yet the hope for many Tasmanians of years past—that one or other of the major parties at a national level would act to end the madness of old-growth logging—vanished with Kevin Rudd's Labor Party green light to Gunns. No one could look to a political system now so hopelessly frightened by—and enmeshed with—the woodchipping lobby to effect change. After a decade of the most pro-corporation national government Australia has ever had, neither major political party has the courage or integrity to stand up to a rogue corporation.

And it is Gunns' determination to do whatever it must to continue old-growth logging that may just condemn both it and Tasmania to a savage vortex: given the history of dependence on government subsidies and the alacrity with which both major parties grant them, Gunns' ability to always shift losses on to others—the government, its workers—means that the company may well continue to prosper. But the price of maintaining the necessary political support is high and ever higher: it demands an ever more determined manipulation of public opinion, an ever more ruthless treatment of public opposition, and an ever more determined duchessing and policing of political parties.

For that reason, more Tasmanians are demanding a royal commission into the Tasmanian old-growth logging industry and its relationship with both major political parties. It may find nothing untoward has taken place. It may find something criminal has occurred. It may even find at heart something far more disturbing: that the boundary between what is illegal and what is unethical has now vanished in Australia, and that the spectre that now haunts Australia is not that of an omnipotent state but of a ruthless corporation, beholden to nothing but its own bottom line, inhibited by nobody, liberated by the failure of contemporary politics.

Nothing less than a major investigation with special powers can now clear away the stench that surrounds this industry and shames Australia. Without such an investigation nothing will change except for the worse, and this rape of Tasmania will continue until one day, like so much else precious, its great forests will belong only to myth. Tasmanians will be condemned to endure the final humiliation: bearing dumb witness to the great lie that delivers wealth to a handful elsewhere, poverty to many of them, and death to their future as the last of these extraordinary places is sacrificed to the woodchippers' greed. Beautiful places, holy places, lost not only to them, but to the world, forever.

And in a world where it seems everything can

be bought, all that will remain are ghosts briefly mocking memory: a ream of copying paper in a Japanese office and a man fern in an English garden. And then they too will be gone.

The Telegraph (London)
April 2007

The Monthly
May 2007

The Road to Kinglake

'THEY CALL IT FIRE FREEZE,' she said.

I looked up at the tree branches bowed and twig ends extended, the leaves forced horizontal as though a great gale were blowing. Yet the air was still. And the charred tree was dead, and had been dead since the apocalypse of Saturday.

Then, as the furnace breath of the fire roared through the trees, such was its ferocious heat that it sucked all moisture out of the branches and leaves, freezing them in this final position of life. And yet the leaves didn't burn.

Four days later, as we climbed the road to Kinglake, the landscape appeared not so much incinerated—as might be expected—as irradiated. As though some death ray had passed through at incomprehensible speed, blobs and runs of aluminium knuckled the bitumen of the road leading into the town that was being described in the media as having vanished in the firestorm.

And yet not everything was dead. Fifty metres down the road from the burnt-out wreck of a dual cab was a green, living tree. Three white goats pocked a black paddock.

The town was still closed off to all bar residents, emergency services, forensic investigators and some media. To get there, you drove up a range through a forest of charred trees rising like an endless nail bed, occasionally broken by yellow-coated CFA volunteers putting out smoking stumps, repairmen clearing roads of fallen trees, replacing power lines and poles, and a quickening rhythm of charred houses and burnt-out cars.

Nothing was as you might expect. Next to writhing twists of ash-white tin that were once homes were houses still standing, with large trees a few metres from their doorway. And at the heart of the destruction, the centre of Kinglake had somehow survived.

Here, the atmosphere of a country show seemed to prevail, with what seemed excessive activity: sprawling parking, container shopfronts and barbecues, the endlessly dividing and reforming circles of people. But it was not a country show.

The smell of onions and burgers frying threw a fatty blanket over the pungent ash of the air, but only if you stood close. The container offices housed government agencies, insurers, emergency services. The people were CFA volunteers, emergency workers, families, old friends near and distant. Survivors, mostly. Their talk was not the squeals and screams of the fairground, but the low murmur of something else. And they moved slowly, as if in wonderment.

'Everyone,' said one woman, 'knows someone who is dead.'

The small run of shops in the town centre had opened their doors and beneath the verandahs were palettes of potatoes, watermelons, tomatoes, cordials and signs saying, 'FREE FOOD. TAKE WHAT YOU NEED.'

Not everyone did. A woman tells me that some whose homes were not destroyed feel they shouldn't help themselves. Everyone feels something, but no one can say what it is, and all seem marked by some odd tenderness of being.

People greeted each other not cursorily, nor quickly, but in what seemed slow awe. An emotion as large and incomprehensible as the ash-strewn world itself seemed to engulf them. People stopped, looked at one another, held each other in—what?—gratitude, relief, grief, love? Whatever it was, if you came from elsewhere it felt wrong to try to pretend you could enter it.

The media were looking for the tragic death

story, the heroic survival story, something that might do some justice to that terrible hushed emotion that seemed to swallow up everything. They ringed one couple telling their dramatic story of escape, of how they passed cars already burnt out with bodies inside. But they did not want to talk about it.

The journos did it because it was their job and they were trying to do their job well, and they did it because they needed a single story that might speak of all these other things: the luck, the serendipity of life and death, the feeling of a world no longer controllable. But no story would do.

'It's the same story,' whispered a frustrated TV-news reporter to his cameraman. 'We've had all this already.' And maybe it was and maybe they had. But no story, no detail, no utterance summed up any of it.

The woman who smiled at me so beautifully, who held my forearm as though I was the one in need of solace, comfort, said, 'I'm all right. You shouldn't talk to me. I feel so —'

She halted, as though the next word were somehow wrong to say.

'Guilty,' she then said. She clipped the end of the word. 'We survived,' she said. 'We're all right,' she continued more quickly. 'There are others over there you should talk to.' She pointed down an alley where clothes were being distributed. Her hand was shaking on my forearm. She forced a smile, excused herself and walked away.

There was already a lot of expert opinion in the media on why the fires had happened. That it was the fault of greenies, or people who had left too late or had no fire plan. But in Kinglake there seemed few certainties. Why some had died was as unexplainable as why others had lived. Other than luck, which was the word that came up again and again.

The man who had been fighting a fire away from the town on Saturday told me he did not know if his wife was safe until the day after, the three plastic cups of instant coffee he held beginning to tremble as he spoke.

'That's her,' he said, motioning with a bowing head over my shoulder.

'We were lucky,' he said. And he walked over to two women, and one put her arms around his neck and burst into tears and could not stop crying, as though they were seeing each other again for the first time after that dreadful Saturday night.

Everyone knew someone who had lost someone, and everyone had a story, and every story was the tip of something huge and beyond any telling or hearing. It all made as little sense as the way day had turned to night, the roar beyond description as the fire approached, the tar melting, the trees falling and cars smashing, the people panicking, the people even more puzzlingly simply watching, the sight of the dead; the inexplicable, even ridiculous, way you might live.

There was the couple who ran across the road and took shelter in the Kinglake West milk bar—a brick building—as the fire barrelled down the main road toward them, only to look down in their relief and see gas bottles. They turned, ran back across the road to their house, and just as they made it to the other side the bottles exploded, blowing out the back of the shop.

Everyone had a story, even those who were not there, like the man who said he'd had a blue with his wife. She'd left on the Friday, and he decided midday Saturday to go down to Melbourne to work for the day. Now they were alive, reunited, and aware of the irony that had allowed this to be so.

'I was a street kid for most of my life,' said another man. 'Moved here four years ago and it's the best place I've ever lived. I felt part of a community, first time ever, such a good place.'

I saw a moment of fire freeze, one world trapped in death, another yet to start.

'You know what I mean?' he said. But I didn't really.

All around us were people frying onions and hamburgers and sorting clothes, people ash-smeared and fire-exhausted, people still to grieve and people unable to be grateful, people reaching out to each other, people looking out for one another and discovering the extraordinary in themselves.

'Such a good place,' he said again. 'You know?'

Beyond us the police teams were turning over tin, turning up more and more dead, yet everywhere I looked I saw only the living helping the living, people holding people, people giving to people. At the end of an era of greed, at a time when all around are crises beyond understanding and seemingly without end, here, in the heart of our apocalypse, I had not been ready for the shock of such goodness.

The Monthly
March 2009

The Flanatta

This recipe could not be simpler, requires no kneading, and makes a beautiful loaf. It is a version of the ciabatta loaf, a seemingly old-fashioned crusty and holey bread reputedly invented by a Venetian baker in the 1960s. The heart of the recipe is a wildly wet dough (80 per cent water as opposed to the more traditional 60 per cent) and a long proving time. The lengthy rising is what gives this loaf great taste and texture. To simulate a steam oven it makes use of a cast-iron casserole in which the bread bakes in its own steam. This produces a most lovely crust, so difficult to otherwise obtain with a domestic oven. You can use a French-style Le Creuset or some such, but a $40 camp oven does the job better and you run no risk of destroying expensive enamelled cookware.

The Ingredients

500 g plain flour
400 ml cold water
1 tsp salt
1/3 tsp dry yeast

The Work

1. Mix the yeast, salt and flour together in a bowl.
2. Add the cold water and mix with your hand until you have a thick batter.
3. Cover the bowl with cling wrap. Leave to rise for between 16 and 24 hours.
4. Thickly flour a bench and pour out the dough. Lightly flour the sticky mass and then push and prod it into the biggest square you can. Pick up the corners, stretch them out and fold them inwards, one on top of the other until you have a lump-like loaf. Leave for an hour.
5. Place the cast-iron casserole in the oven and preheat to 240°C.
6. Carefully take the very hot casserole out of the oven, remove the lid, dust the base with flour, and drop your dough into the centre.
7. Replace the lid and bake for 30 minutes.
8. Remove the lid, and bake for another 15–20 minutes until the bread is well browned.
9. Cool on a rack for an hour before cutting.
10. Find a kitchen table. Fill it with friends. Bottles. Stories. And share. With or without a breadknife.